في ذكرى

مارك لينز

NAGUIB MAHFOUZ

On Literature and Philosophy

The Non-Fiction Writing of Naguib Mahfouz Volume I

Translated by Aran Byrne

GINGKO
LIBRARY

تمت ترجمة هذا الكتاب بمساعدة صندوق منحة الترجمة
المقدمة من معرض الشارقة الدولي للكتاب

This book has been translated with the assistance
of the Sharjah International Book Fair Translation
Grant Fund

First published in the United Kingdom in 2016 by
Gingko Library
70 Cadogan Place, London SW1X 9AH

Originally published in Arabic as *Ḥawla l-Adab wa-l-Falsafa*
Copyright © 2015 Dar Al Masriah Al Lubnaniah, Cairo

Translation Copyright © Aran Byrne, 2016

ISBN 978-1-909942-77-6
eISBN 978-1-909942-78-3

Typeset in Optima by MacGuru Ltd

Printed in Spain

www.gingkolibrary.com
@gingkolibrary

Contents

Introduction

by Rasheed El-Enany

Scholars and devoted readers of Naguib Mahfouz in English will be delighted to see in print this volume containing a good number of his early essays collected for the first time between the two covers of a book. Readers of Arabic have beat them to that pleasure in 2003 when the collection first saw the light when Mahfouz still had three years to live. Most of the essays belong to the 1930s decade with a few from the 1940s. When Mahfouz started writing those essays, the first of which in this volume dates back to October 1930, he was still an undergraduate student reading philosophy at Cairo University, then known as Fu'ad I University. At that time he had not written any fiction yet and little did he know that he was destined to become the real father of the genre in Arabic and renowned novelist and Nobel laureate with an international following. He still had a few years in which to settle what he often referred to as the fight between philosophy and literature over his soul in favour of the latter. The first of the articles in this volume was published in *Al-Majalla al-Jadida* – the very same publication that 9 years later, in 1939, was to publish in a supplement his first novel, The Mockery of Fate, or *Khufu's Wisdom,* as the title was rendered, many years later, in its English translation. Edited by the progressive writer, Salama Musa (1887–1958), who advocated secularism and socialism during a period that has in retrospect come to be regarded as the peak of liberal thinking in 20th century Egypt, the young Mahfouz appears to have found a natural home for his budding talent, although as this collection shows he also published in other newspapers and literary magazines of the day.

The first essay, titled 'The Demise of Old Beliefs and the Emergence of New Ones' could have been written by Salama Musa himself, whose influence Mahfouz has repeatedly acknowledged. In this inaugural essay, penned by Mahfouz when he was only 19 years old, we find the germination of many a central theme that was to persist with him in his more mature years and to recur time and again in the social and philosophical ideas that inhabit his fiction. This is why this volume is important for the study and understanding of Mahfouz and his development as a writer and thinker. Most of the existing scholarship on Mahfouz has not benefited from these early essays because, as already indicated, until 2003, when Mahfouz had already been a world famous Nobel laureate since 1988 with his achievement largely behind him, the essays had remained scattered in long-defunct literary magazines hard to come by even in libraries. Nor to the best of my knowledge was there a list of them that could usefully be used as a guide by a determined researcher. Above all, Mahfouz himself was not a great help in the matter. He was indifferent about the essays as mere juvenilia and had routinely declined propositions to collect and publish them. When he finally relented and the essays became available, it was not difficult to see at one and the same time why he had thwarted efforts to collect them for so long, but also why he was wrong to do so.

The essays have little value in their own right today, though they may have served a good purpose indeed as part of the ongoing endeavour of public enlightenment undertaken by the intellectual class of the day in that golden age of liberal thought in Egypt. They are mostly expository essays engaging with western thought and ideologies, whether philosophical, political, social, literary or religious, with the majority being on philosophy and its erstwhile satellite disciplines of psychology and philology – clearly a reflection of his own immersion in the subject he specialised in as a university student, but also of the ideas and their major exponents that preoccupied him as they did others at the time and that he wanted to share with his readership. There is hardly any original contribution there, while at present much of the content, if not dated, is taken for granted and has long been in the public arena. Where the interest lies today in reading these essays is in

tracing Mahfouz's own intellectual sympathies with regard to the thinking and ideologies he expounds. With the benefit of hindsight, scholars
of Mahfouz can recognise in these essays the origins of much of what
was later to become his intellectual hallmark.

To go back to his first essay in the volume, 'The Demise of Old
Beliefs and the Emergence of New Ones' – this for instance immediately reveals the secularist Mahfouz who rejects the 'sacredness' of any
beliefs, and welcomes 'the commotion' brought about by new ideas,
because that is how 'progress' is achieved. This is the nascent Mahfouz
who will write decades later a controversial novel, called The Children
of our Alley (1959) (later translated as Children of Gebelawi and again
as Children of the Alley), which will lead to an attempt on his life by a
religious fanatic, and in which he casts old prophets of Judaism, Christianity and Islam in a thinly disguised allegory, as nothing more than
social reformers, whose role and that of religion was replaced by belief
in science in modern times. In that same essay we also see the beginnings of Mahfouz's belief in socialism as humanity's best answer to
date to social ills. These thoughts, concerned with socialism, secularism and the role of religion in modern society, were soon after to find
their concrete representations in Mahfouz's earliest realistic novels, set
in the Cairo of the 1930s and 1940s, Khan al-Khalili (1945) and The
New Cairo (1946), translated as Cairo Modern.

The majority of the essays consist of sweeping summaries of philosophical schools, worthy of a concise encyclopaedia: Socrates, Plato,
Aristotle, the Sophists, the Stoics, the Epicureans, the Neo-Platonists
are all there, as are Descartes, Kant, David Hume, John Stuart Mill,
Bergson, William James, Pavlov, and plenty others, including scores
of less resonant names. Interestingly, indeed bewilderingly, in all these
hosts of names of thinkers and theorisers and in all his expositions
of a multitude of philosophical schools, there is not to be found any
reference to Islamic philosophy or any of its major figures, whose influence on western philosophy and role as conduits of Greek thought
to Europe as it awakened from medievalism into the Renaissance, is
well-established; we do not come here, not for once, across such illus-
trious names as al-Kindi, al-Farabi, Avicenna, the Brethren of Purity,

Ibn Arabi, Averroes etc. No programme of study of philosophy could afford not to stop at those figures, no more then than now. How then can we explain that the young Mahfouz, who seemed to take it upon himself to educate his 1930s and 40s readers in philosophy, passing on to them in simplified manner what he had been studying in his specialised academic discipline, that he completely overlooked, consciously or unconsciously, to enlighten them on the Muslim contribution to philosophy? What inferences can be made from this glaring omission? I can think of none except that he was wholeheartedly immersed in western thought and the European model as the gateway to modernity. In the learned milieu of the day that formed the background to Mahfouz's intellectual formation, there were two conflicting tendencies: one revivalist in nature harking back to the Arabo-Islamic roots of Egypt, and another that took pride in Egypt's ancient civilisation on the one hand and saw its future, on the other, in the embracement of the European model, bypassing largely its Arabo-Islamic phase. Mahfouz was undoubtedly an adherent of the latter. Several of his early short stories and more importantly his first three full-length novels, were historical ones, set in Ancient Egypt; indeed part of a huge project to document the entire history of Ancient Egypt in a series of grand narratives after the Scottish model of Walter Scott, but which he abandoned after the first three instances in favour of realism and the depiction of the contemporary social scene. This early shift to the contemporary scene came only to confirm his already recognisable alignment: in his early realistic novels such as *Khan al-Khalili* and *Cairo Modern,* onward to The Trilogy, published in the 1940s and 50s, he was churning out novels that delineated the conflict raging over Egypt's soul between advocates of modernity inspired by the European model and the backward-looking revivalist inclination, often represented by the then rising socio-political force of the Muslim Brotherhood: time and again his authorial sympathy was never in doubt. This is the only context I can advance as a way of understanding the absence of any treatment of Islamic philosophy amidst the wide and far-reaching array of those early philosophic essays. In his much later work, starting from the 1960s onwards, some Islamic influences were to be witnessed in his work, but only those of Sufism, as a literary trope for the renunciation of life, an abandonment of the pressing issues of politics, society and the tribulations of personal life. However, Sufism was always shown not to work – an escapist strategy, an opting out with negative consequences for both the individual and society, a fascinating alternative to engagement but one that offers no salvation.

An almost arbitrary example to show the consistency of Mahfouz's intellectual position can be found in his essay on 'The development of philosophy in the pre-Socratic era'. Even in such a quick summary of a wide topic, the conclusion to which he draws the attention of the reader at the end is telling: belief in human progress and the elevation of reason as the means to understand nature: 'how the human mind was, little by little, freed from materiality ... and how these philosophies reached the heights of abstract interpretation which only the rational mind could achieve.' This early admiration of reason and rationality will remain at the heart of Mahfouz's preoccupation with the metaphysical questions he explores in his fiction, where belief in the metaphysical is never reconciled to reason and the facts of empirical reality (Consider for instance, his 1975 'treatise' on God and belief in the disguise of a novel, called *Heart of the Night*.) Not all his philosophical essays however are necessarily revealing about his intellectual position at the time of writing or later. Many of them are simply instructive in nature, with no apparent purpose but the education of the reader in simple terms with regard to important philosophers and their systems of thought. This for instance is the case with the two essays immediately following the one in hand, i.e. 'The philosophy of Socrates' and 'Plato and his philosophy'; such is the case with many others too.

One feeling the reader comes out with from reading Mahfouz's essays on philosophy is that if he had not been a great novelist, he would have been a great teacher. He is adroit at introducing and expounding ideas, observing chronology, making connections, exposing weaknesses and strengths before coming to conclusions, while remaining neutral most of the time, allowing the reader to think for himself. He is also a great simplifier who is able to make such a difficult subject as philosophy accessible to the lay reader. The way his essays are so tightly structured, built one paragraph over another, one thought flowing from the previous and leading to the next, the sense of organisation, of control over his material, of knowing where he started and where he is heading – all herald the great architect of the plots of his novels that we were to come to know later. It is as if the mind that knew how to structure a work like The Trilogy – with its roughly 1500 pages, scores of characters, themes and sub-plots, never losing control, tying up all loose ends – demonstrated its organisational force in those early short but ramifying essays.

Despite the title of this collection, there is only a handful of essays on literature as such and some of those are reviews of books published at the time, or inconsequential sketches of literary figures he admired, e.g. Anton Chekhov; the numerical balance is overwhelmingly tipped in favour of philosophy. There is only one essay that merits a pause. It bears the title 'Art and Culture' and was published in *al-Majalla al-Jadida* again in 1936, nearly two years after Mahfouz had obtained his degree in philosophy and nearing a reconciliation of his internal tug-of-war between philosophy and literature. We see him here addressing some of the theoretical questions that he was later to resolve in his creative writing. Uppermost in his mind was the question of what could be considered the proper subject matter of art? Feelings and emotional experiences only? Or could intellectual issues and scientific knowledge of the world and the whole universe inform literary writing too? As he puts it, 'should art remain pure for the sake of art, free from anything except emotion and instinct? Or, should it be possible for art to deal additionally with subjects of the rational mind, the branches of knowledge, and pronouncements of philosophy associated with it?' He goes on to expound further the view that art should be limited to matters of emotion; a view that we now know he was not to endorse in his own art in later years: 'In this manner, literature becomes a simple depiction of natural emotions, such as love, pain, hatred, and pleasure, while anything other than that, i.e. the objectives of the rational mind and its subject matters, will be seen as being in excess of true art, and an addiction to it will degrade its essence and dispossess it of its beauty and its exaltedness.' However, as the essay progresses, the young Mahfouz drops unceremoniously any pretence to neutrality in his exposition of the two opposed views. He proclaims himself unequivocally in the camp that throws in everything in art: instinct and feelings by all means, but also intellectual issues and the fruit of scientific knowledge. The artist who is acquainted with the history of mankind, its intellectual, scientific, social and issues and achievements, will be better equipped to express himself, and project his emotional experiences in art, because, 'he will possess the means to behold what is hidden and see worlds that he would not comprehend anything of were it not for ... [the] sciences. The instinctive mind is far baser than that mind whose parts are illuminated by knowledge. The creative output of the former, no matter how talented or equipped with genius, cannot rise above that of the latter if equally equipped with aptitude and talent.'

That Mahfouz should be preoccupied at the time he was with this dichotomy, which today sounds a trifle contrived, is not surprising in the context of the literary taste prevailing in his day, which was dominated by narrative prose of a highly ornamental nature in style and weepy sentimentality in content, best exemplified by the creations and translations of the idolised stylist of the day, Mustafa Lutfi al-Manfluti (1876–1924), one of whose books was appropriately titled, *Tears* (1916), though collections with other titles were no less tearfully maudlin. Clearly Mahfouz knew what he wanted to do from early on and it was nothing like that. He was setting out his intellectual position here in theory, years before he even wrote his first novel. But when the time came, he was to become an artist of the 'latter' type; the type whose art is informed by the full spectrum of human knowledge. In his fiction we encounter countless ideologies, ancient and modern, political, philosophical, religious, sociological, psychological, as well as scientific discoveries, past and present. However, they are not there in their abstract form, in the manner we have encountered some of them in the essays of this volume for instance; rather, they are assimilated in his characters and their words and actions. They are not superimposed but emanate from the texture of his artistic creations. We see ideas as they become human force and change the lives of individuals and societies happily or tragically. That is how intellectual knowledge works in art, and it seems that was what Mahfouz understood in the abstract from the start before he began to practice it in his creation. And it will be interesting for any reader approaching the work of Mahfouz chronologically to note how this process had happened gradually, as the writer perfected his tools and polished his talent. Political and social ideologies in his very early novels, e.g. *Khan al-Khalili* and *Cairo Modern,* are easily identifiable and characters seem to be there to carry them and become exponents of conflicting ideas and social currents; in other terms, the ideologies that Mahfouz as writer supported or opposed are floating on the surface rather than blended with the texture of the work. That was to change as the novelist's career progressed.

Perhaps Mahfouz was not accurate when he spoke of his early inner conflict between philosophy and literature being finally resolved in favour of the latter. The truth is there was no victor in that conflict, but a reconciliation, a peace accord in which philosophy agreed to hide behind the guise of literature and proclaim itself only through metaphor.

February, 2016
Rasheed El-Enany
Professor of Arabic and Comparative Literature,
Doha institute for Graduate Studies
Professor Emeritus of Modern Arabic Literature, University of Exeter

Translator's Preface

On Literature and Philosophy, is a translation of another book by the same title, *Ḥawla l-Adab wa-l-Falsafa*,[1] which comprises early, non-fiction essays of Naguib Mahfouz that were originally published in various Egyptian journals between 1930 and 1945 – though the majority are dated prior to 1937. With regards to the translation, I have generally inclined towards fidelity to the original essays, as opposed to producing a more corrective translation. At times, the thought and writing in these early essays lack sophistication, and much of this has been reproduced in the translation, as will be apparent. The reasoning for this is that the importance of these essays, as I see it, lies more in their value as historical documents – which can provide insights into the historical milieu, and the mind of Mahfouz himself – rather than in their value as informative pieces about philosophy and other topics, though would almost certainly have been the original, underlying intention behind their publication.

Textual errors and defects in Arabic are not uncommon in the original collection. These may derive from the sources Mahfouz was using at the time, or they may be due to failures occurring during the editing processes prior to their publication. Obvious typographical errors have been corrected where they have been identified, while factual errors have generally been left in the text but footnoted. Where Mahfouz has used quoted material in his essays he did not provided any reference to his sources. Some of these quotations appear to me to be quite odd

---

1 Full reference: Mahfouz, Naguib, *Ḥawla l-Adab wa-l-Falsafa*, Cairo, 2003

in the original Arabic, and probably incorrect, but without knowing his sources it can be difficult to offer alternative renderings. In light of this, his quotations have been reproduced for the most part, even where the correctness of these seems questionable.

A significant problem in the essays is that while Mahfouz discusses a great many individuals, particularly in the essays dealing with philosophical themes, he very often gives only the surname, without providing the forename of the individual in question. The matter of confirming whom he is referring to was sometimes further confounded by the use of different, and incorrect, spellings in the texts for the same persons: the name 'Thucydides', for example, usually spelled now as *thūsīdīdīs* (and sometimes *thiyūsīdīdiz*) is written as *tiyūkīdīd*, and subsequently as *īthīdīd*, in one paragraph.[2] While very well-known personages, such as Thucydides, were fairly easy to identify and correct, for the most part, there were other instances where, not being provided with a forename, made it difficult to identify the person being cited with any great certainty. One example of this is where Mahfouz discusses someone by the name of 'Marshall' (*mārshāl*), since no forename is provided, and since context, which might have provided greater clues to the person's identity, is slight, it remains a matter of speculation as to who exactly this Marshall is.[3] Furthermore, there were also a few instances where I was unable to even know the correct spelling of the name cited, never mind identify whom it referred to. Such instances have been footnoted.

Another difficulty encountered in translating these essays pertains generally to Mahfouz' use of language, particularly with regard to the philosophical pieces. Some instances are more quaint than problematic. However, problematic instances do occur where precision in language is lacking. Mahfouz' focus is almost entirely upon the Western philosophical tradition, as opposed to Islamic philosophy, where much of the Arabic terminology would have been more or less fixed. While he does use precise Western terms, be they Arabicised loan words

---

2 Mahfouz, Naguib, *Ḥawla l-Adab wa-l-Falsafa*, Cairo, 2003, p. 66
3 Mahfouz, Naguib, *Ḥawla l-Adab wa-l-Falsafa*, Cairo, 2003, p. 112

– such as *trūbīzm* ('tropism'), for example – or words given in their original European language, such as 'reflexes', [4] he frequently conveys modern Western terms using Arabic words that do not always closely correspond. Complex ideas are often conveyed using what appears to be improvised or simplistic language, and care is not always taken to precisely, and consistently, differentiate between certain concepts. Perhaps the most difficult instance of this is his general use of the word *nafs* throughout to convey a number of quite different, and distinct, concepts such as 'soul', 'psyche', 'mind', 'self', 'essence', and others. Generally speaking, where possible, I have tried to translate terms according to context, such as the historical periods they may pertain to, or in light of the philosophers with whom they are associated.

I should also note that the punctuation in the translation differs from that used in the Arabic, but this is to be expected, and I have tried to ensure that it does not distort the meaning of the original text. I have also changed the paragraphing in the translation; Mahfouz often uses very brief paragraphs, sometimes consisting of only one or two sentences. I have tended to amalgamate smaller units into larger ones where these are related to one another, since the intervention of such edits has very little impact upon the actual meaning of the texts. Lastly, I am grateful to Russell Harris and Rasheed El-Enany for their advice, and their useful suggestions regarding some of the more difficult aspects involved in the translation.

Aran Byrne
January 2016

---

4 Both examples can be found here: Mahfouz, Naguib, *Ḥawla l-Adab wa-l-Falsafa*, Cairo, 2003, p. 112

The Demise of Old Beliefs and the Emergence of New Ones[1]

According to Gustave Le Bon, the ancient civilisations were built on foundations of firm beliefs, regardless of whether these were religious or political. Furthermore, these civilisations were strong and enduring precisely because the beliefs upon which they had been founded were deeply rooted in people's minds. Occupying such a central position, these beliefs were never questioned or exposed to criticism; this would have bred scepticism and doubt. They comprised errors and superstitions that were entirely irrational, but which, for the most part, gave reassurance to those who adopted them. However, if doubts ever did emerge concerning a given belief – that is, a conviction upon which the civilisation was based – then this would inevitably lead to that civilisation's demise. Indeed, this is precisely what we are witnessing today in our own era: those beliefs that have been held for generations have been gradually eroded and slowly ripped out from underneath us.

Man, in his nature, and by virtue of the religious feeling which fills his being, always seeks to believe in that which will give him faith and deliverance. It is for this reason that he can be seen to embrace social movements and adopt certain political views. He throws himself into his cause just as his forebears did before him in the cause of God or that of an emperor. However, with regard to these modern views and movements, none of them have yet become established within us like

---

1 Article from *al-Majalla al-Jadida* October 1930

those of old; they have not left their mark upon the sacred religious character, which, when questioned or criticised, causes unbelief and a loss of faith. We are now living through an era in which beliefs and convictions that have long been held are disappearing and dying out, while other views and beliefs – which are not yet fully established – are replacing them. In this sense, this is an era of commotion and indecision like no other in history. There is commotion in the clash of ideas, there is struggle for a certain way of life, for the victory and establishment of a given doctrine, and there is indecision regarding acceptance of the various doctrines, many of which are in opposition to one another. The stronger doctrines seek to eradicate the weaker, declining ones. In this way, we see how as soon as a book promoting some doctrine appears, another one is published in response, mocking the former's ideas and attacking it in the harshest manner, then, in no time at all, another one is authored which proposes a third, middle way between the other two opposing views, and so on.

There is no doubt that a stable civilisation and way of life, in which matters run their natural course, is preferable to this alarming commotion. Nevertheless, I do not grieve the approaching demise of obsolete beliefs, nor do I call upon intellectuals to cease questioning and criticising them so that the sacredness and prestige of these beliefs might be preserved, just so that we might live calm and untroubled lives. I adopt this course because I hold the view that this commotion is a natural and unavoidable phenomenon which advances civilisation, just as I also believe it to be an expression of intellectual development – something that occurs from time to time and which gives us a true gauge of our progress. When old convictions become unpalatable, the intellect will destroy them. This occurs when rationality reaches a point where its criticism of these convictions necessarily occurs. In this case, consideration no longer enters into it and there no choice in the matter. It is as inevitable as the appearance of grey hair on a man's head when he grows old. One cannot resist the movement toward renewal anymore than one can defy the laws of nature.

Furthermore, I am not pessimistic concerning the loss of faith in old beliefs, nor do I accept this will lead to the destruction of the world, as many pessimists claim. Rather, I view this process as nothing more than the renewal of the foundation, or the construction of a solid, new one. I would not rush in building this. Instead, I believe that we should let time and evolution take their course: they are the agents that will realise what we dream of on our behalf, without us resorting to revolutions in order to win what we desire. Indeed, revolutions may appear to force time forward, but in reality they cause nothing but destruction and disorder – consequences that serve only put us back to the start.

This cursory depiction of how our beliefs have been challenged helps us to explain, to some extent, the alarming developments that can also be seen to have taken place in literature. In the past, when the old beliefs prevailed and held sway over people feelings and existence – whether they were from the upper classes or the lower ones – the litterateurs, with their books and narratives, gave truer expression to those beliefs that influenced them. To be persuaded of this point, all one has to do skim through some of the weighty volumes that have been composed since the advent of Islam which were written to explain the meaning of religious texts, or to compile the sayings of the prophet and interpret them. Indeed, it would be enough to read the collected works of certain poets who concerned themselves solely with composing verse about the wisdom found in religion, with praising the prophet, and with extolling the divine.

As with religion, the same holds true of politics and society; many books and narratives have been written in support of a doctrine, to promote a certain principle, or to spread a claim. When the old beliefs began to perish, and when the light of the rational mind began to assert power over them, it laid bare their flaws and revealed their disgraces which had lived and taken root within people's minds over the generations as though they were self-evident truths that were beyond dispute. When doubt came to replace faith, the writers were influenced by the change. Writers have been the greatest supporters and propagators of the new. They compose books which attack that which is outdated and try to bring about its demise, freeing us from enthrallment and enslavement to it. A result of this is that there are now many books and narratives which, when read, cause us to have doubts about the past, and the opinions and beliefs that used to be held. Many promote new ideologies such as socialism, internationalism, and others.

We should observe here how all of these new ideologies aspire to the achievement of global unity and an end to national divisions. In this sense they are in agreement with the old faiths, such as Christianity and Islam. However, some of these new doctrines go further: they call for an end to class divisions.

Now, if I had to offer a prediction about which doctrine will triumph over the others, I would say, or rather, I should like to say, that it will be socialism. This is because its promises appeal to the hearts of the disaffected, the discontented, and the poor, who represent the vast majority of the world's human population. Furthermore, socialism is appealing because it seeks to remedy the tangible gap which has arisen due to scientific progress, and the emergence of new inventions and machines, and because it presents a middle way between two systems about which the religious complain: communism and individualism. From these two doctrines socialism has taken the good parts, and rejected the apparent defects, of each. Beyond this, there are many other reasons why I am almost certain that the future belongs to socialism, but I am not presently concerned with exploring them further here.

I should mention, however, that the bliss promised by socialism is a worldly one: it pertains to this life, not to a hereafter. This is one reason that it might be unable fulfil its promises in their entirety. In this case, its most enthusiastic and active supporters will be defeated. However, we must also not forget that perfection in this world is an impossibility, and that, even if socialism can't lead us to a state of bliss, after which there will be no more search, nevertheless, it can still improve the conditions in which we live. Socialism does not represent the conclusion and the cessation of social evolution; the aspiration for something better will always drive us to seek whatever might give us comfort and happiness.

On this topic I would like to say that, if the hope I have in socialism turns out to be misplaced, to a greater or lesser extent, then that does not mean that I would seek to retreat back to the prior, bad state – by which I mean the present one. Rather, any setback would cause my faith in change and evolution to increase, because it is only through this process that ideas and beliefs, such as socialism itself, come into being.

Women and Public Office[1]

The day in which we will see women occupying jobs in government in similar numbers to men – and in which we will be able say that women are now equal to men in having the right to hold governmental positions – is a long way off. To understand the consequences that will arise from giving women the right to hold public office, we must envisage a society in which the great majority of females are employed, or studying with the aim of becoming employed.

The first consequence we need consider is that, by conceding that women are fit to hold positions of employment like men, we will be granting recognition to one of their most significant demands. The result of this will be that, if there are women writers, doctors, engineers and judges, then there will also be women members of parliament and women ministers. Here the reader must note that the scenario I am discussing pertains to the distant future – indeed, perhaps the very distant future. That is to say, I am talking about a time in which the majority of women will have occupations, and, in particular, in which women will hold positions in government, which is the issue in question.

The second consequence we should consider is the impact that such developments would have on the family. The status of a young woman who is employed would change: she would become a valued and respected member of her family. A young, working woman would gain complete independence to determine the course of her life. In this event, she would represent a source of income for the family, instead

1 Article from *al-Siyasa al-Usbu'iya* 11 October 1930

of being a burden on her father as before. Furthermore, a woman's ideas about marriage would change: marriage would no longer be her sole aim in life. From this it follows that she would refuse to marry just anyone who sought her hand in marriage – as though she were some cheap item to be sold off to the first buyer that comes along – rather, she would now have the option to choose the man she thinks suitable, the one whom she deems worthy of her.

Where such things to come about, the felicity existing between a married couple would be constantly under attack. The wife might be transferred to work in the north of the country and the husband transferred to a different place in the south, in which case they would be separated. In such wretched circumstances they would each find a thousand reasons to justify getting a divorce. The sanctity of marriage would be lost and its contract would become a trivial thing to be treated lightly, something that could be broken as though the vow to honour it was of no importance.

I should also draw attention to a problem which many of the civilised countries complain about: the problem of unemployment. There is no doubt that competition between young men and women to enter the workplace will result in an increase of graduates who are out of work. Furthermore, because their education is theoretical in nature, and because their learning in the various fields of knowledge inclines them to self-conceit, they will be incapable of taking up other kinds of work for which there is a demand. It is feared that they will be returned to society and rise up against its laws.

The Development of Philosophy in the Pre-Socratic Era[1]

The concerns of primitive man were limited to the things in his surrounding environment – objects in which he sought some use or other for his survival. His skill found expression in copying and imitating, in roaring and dancing. Many eras passed by, however, and during this time humans developed language, by which they could communicate with one another. Now, when language developed into a tool for thought, and as man began to think more, he increasingly used his mind and imagination to interpret life and death. He faced many dangers in the world; he saw perils in the wild and savage beasts, and he heard them in the lightning's thunder, which disturbed him in his dreams. In his primitive interpretations of such things we find the first seed of philosophy, which gradually and continually grew over the course of different eras. This reveals to us the different stages of development through which human thought passed; indeed, the history of philosophy is, in reality, the history of the rational, human mind itself.

We are talking here about Greek, Pre-Socratic philosophy, which, in its beginnings, manifested a primitive, simple type of thinking, but which gradually developed into scientific thinking based upon the use of methods and evidence. It does not matter if this philosophy attained brilliance without having been influenced by ideas coming from abroad, or, on the contrary, if it was derived from another philosophy that did come from another country, such as Persia, for example, because the

---

1 Article from *al-Majalla al-Ma'rifa* August 1931

human intellect, in its development, ascends one staircase. Similarly, we can correctly view the philosophy that we are presently discussing as an example, and a mode, of thinking in its early stages, that, step by step, would develop into sound, logical thinking.

The principles behind existence preoccupied early thinkers. We can see that nature, and its various phenomena, stimulated their thinking. Initially, they conceived that the primary cause for the world was something physical, something tangible. This was the philosophical theory of the Ionians. The Ionian philosopher Thales asserted that water was the basis of everything, that all things emerge from it, and return to it. He tried to construct his theory upon scientific principles, and it is by virtue of this that he attained his place in the history of philosophy. Other Ionian philosophers disagreed with him; however, they differed only with respect to the particular element which he proposed as being the source of the world, not that the source itself was a perceptible element. In this sense, the disagreement is slight to anyone who looks into the development of human rationality or views its history as a whole. We should note, however, that the Ionian school did make an attempt to break free from the notion of a perceptible element as the source of all things; although the philosopher Anaximander did propose an 'element' of sorts as being the source of the world, he proposed that this was eternal, infinite, and unknowable.

Among adherents of the Pythagorean school, which takes its name from the great philosopher Pythagoras, we find a further challenge against this notion of a perceptible element – this one more bold than its predecessor. The followers of Pythagoras asserted that it cannot be assumed that the source of being is tangible and material; but rather, the correct view is that we should appraise the truth of the source of the world through its various relationships and its measurements. This new theory was not so much concerned with the basic element itself as it was with the perceptual form it took. It did not turn its attention to the elements of water or air, but rather, to the relationships and measurements. When the relationships of things – such as the dimension, size, shape and distances – are expressed as numbers, and since it is impossible for a thing to be in existence if it does not have form and cannot be measured, then it follows that everything is subject to calculation. Thus, the number was considered to be the universal principle for all things. This is the theory which is attributed to Pythagoras; it is sometimes called 'the theory of the number'. However, the question arises, was this new source material or abstract? I do not have an unequivocal answer to this. It is very probable that the attempt to understand this question would have divided the Pythagoreans into two opposing camps.

After the Pythagoreans, the Eleatics – who take their name from the great Greek city, Elea – made a name for themselves in the field of philosophy.[2] They became aware of the philosophy of the Pythagoreans, which we have been discussing. We should keep in mind that the Pythagoreans acknowledged a relationship between the source of being, and time and place, insofar it is not possible to measure a thing which does not have a relationship with time and place. As for the Eleatics, however, they were the first to deny the existence of any link between the source of being, and time and place. This is because they completely divested the notion of materiality. They asserted that it is not possible to comprehend the source of being with the senses; rather, it can only be comprehended through the mind, coining the term 'abstract being'. Among the most important philosophers of this school were Xenophanes, Parmenides and Zeno. Despite the many differences in their philosophies they were in agreement concerning this general principle. However, to discuss them further would be a digression.

We shall now turn from analytical philosophy to constructive philosophy. We have seen how the Eleatics stripped the notion of a source for being of substance, time and place, denying its material nature, and asserting that tangible being was a false phenomenon. Nevertheless, they found that they were forced to discuss the notion of manifest being, and from this emerged a complex philosophical problem for which we find no solution, for according to this philosophy there is no

---

2 The modern-day name of Elea is 'Velia'. It is located in southern Italy in the region of Campania.

relationship between abstract being and tangible being. When Heraclitus determined that the source of being was a union of both abstract and tangible being which we can see and which we partially live in, he stated that it was the nature of things to continually change and that this is a process that never ceases. From this idea put forth by Heraclitus new philosophical questions later emerged: what is the cause for this union, and how does the tangible being come into existence? As for Empedocles, he stated that matter is the source of being, and that force is the source of movement.

Philosophers came to despair about finding causes with which they could explain the nature of material being. Eventually, Anaxagoras came up with the notion that it is the mind that created the world and brought its order into existence. However, like his predecessors, Anaxagoras did not go beyond naturalism, and for this reason he did not comprehend that reason is something beyond material nature. Whatever the case may be, however, it is to the Sophists that we can credit the idea that the mind and nature are distinct from one another, and that it is the mind which the superior of the two.

Sophism was a school that emerged from the questions concerning the senses and the knowledge we derive from them. They attacked the truths which had been arrived at through the use of the senses, that is, knowledge derived from the senses which had been blindly accepted. Generally speaking, they advanced the principle of objective investigation.

This is a brief outline about the development of philosophy prior to the era of Socrates. By this it is hoped that the reader will perceive how the human mind was, little by little, freed from materiality in its attempts to explain the source of manifest, material being, and how these philosophies reached the heights of abstract interpretation which only the rational mind could achieve.

The Philosophy of Socrates[1]

In the last essay I discussed the Pre-Socratic philosophers who turned their attention to the nature of being in order to discover the primary cause behind how something comes into being and from which it gets its various properties. After these philosophers came the Sophists who, through their scepticism, took apart the objective studies of their predecessors. They adopted a form of subjective investigation, which they took as the basis upon which they constructed the principles of ethics and the fundamentals of the sciences. Through this subjectivism they destabilised theories on ethics and disrupted accepted truths. They held that it was entirely permissible for an individual to hold some conviction or other as true even if everyone else disagreed with him, and even if their argument against this individual's conviction was wise and correct!

This philosophy led up to the time of Socrates. He studied it in depth, and from it he developed his own philosophy which, even if it has strong links with the past, is nevertheless different in important ways – indeed, it draws a line over the great human philosophies upon which it is founded and from which it is derived. The method Socrates adopted to propagate his philosophy involved discoursing with people in the street. When he approached them he would question them, feigning ignorance about the given topic, then he would reveal to them their own ignorance by putting doubts in their minds. In this way, through his discourse, he would plant the seeds of true knowledge in

---

1 Article from *al-Majalla al-Ma'rifa* October 1931

those he spoke with. In his discussions with people he did not skirt those questions which had a bearing on life. This is because he did not make a distinction between his philosophical teaching and living itself.

The philosophy of Socrates differed from that of his predecessors because it abandoned the wandering exploration of metaphysics; it did not seek to investigate the darkness of origination. The philosophy of Socrates kept its feet on the ground and engaged the human psyche. The most important of his aims were to know himself and to understand virtue; these are the issues that prompted and preoccupied him. He prided himself on his apparent ignorance; indeed, according to what has been related about him, he credited any intellectual brilliance he manifested to this very ignorance.

In this way he diverged from the philosophy of the Sophists. Like them, he took the human soul as the basis from which truths are to be derived; however, the conclusions he arrived at were in complete opposition to those reached by the Sophists. They had used subjectivism as a means to demolish outward truths, while Socrates used it to affirm them. He would firmly establish the principle of individual thought as having its own truth and independence from that of other individuals; however, he advocated the principle that truths should be arrived at through argument and logical definition. Aristotle said of him, 'Two great achievements can be attributed to Socrates: the use of inference and logical definition ... on these was science built.'

To elucidate this important point it should be stated that Socrates, in his discourses, was moving away from a negative form of inquiry toward an affirmative one. He questioned the people as though he were an ignorant person seeking knowledge, then, if they informed him of their knowledge, he would interrogate them with a barrage questions by which they would become entangled and thrown into confusion. These questions would reveal to his subjects their own ignorance concerning the facts of the matter and demonstrate how certain things which appear to be simple, easy, and in no need of further examination, are, in reality, among the most complicated and difficult of matters. This is the negative aspect, however: in many of Socrates' discourses that have come down to us through Plato the matter ends here.

Thoughts would later dawn on Socrates following his conversations with those he spoke to – thoughts that had not occurred to him during these exchanges. He would interrogate a number of aphorisms, observing their disparities and similarities, how they were connected with one another and where they diverged. Inquiry and argument would then lead him to establish a general concept, such as justice, or happiness, and so forth. This form of disputation aims at establishing a logical definition which is comprehensive, universal, and unassailable. Aristotle said, 'Socrates was concerned with examining the nature of virtue as if it were the principal matter of philosophy. To this end he asked himself, 'What is justice? What is the will?' He did so because he believed that virtue is knowledge.'

Now, when a concept is sound in the workings of all its aspects, it can be considered to be the true being of things. Socrates held the opinion that ethics had a huge influence on both the theoretical world and practical life. He believed that virtue has its origins in knowledge, reason and good judgment. Thus, an act which is carried out blindly and without the use of reason is in conflict with itself, whereas the act which is occasioned by conscious perception will accomplish its goal. From this we can conclude that no harm occurs from the use of reason, or, that no good comes from the absence thereof. Indeed, deficient use of reason is what causes people to fall into the depths of depravity. From this comes the saying that man is benevolent by nature, but he is driven to commit acts of depravity in spite of his reason, and furthermore, he who does evil, but whose crime originates from knowledge and reason, is better than he who does good without having awareness. This is so, because in the latter instance good was done without meaning and without knowledge, and therefore, without virtue. As for the former, evil was done but virtue was nevertheless present and played a role.

The outcome of this idea was logical. It unified all virtues; when someone has done something good, it is, in truth, due to rational intelligence. This leads to the conclusion that this rational intelligence is one whenever it is applied to any subject concerning virtue. Furthermore, there is another, practical outcome: if virtue is knowledge, then it can be taught. Thus, it is possible to propagate it among all individuals through practical application. In this way, Socrates laid the foundation stone for a theory of ethics. He did not attempt to go beyond this, however; he was trying to arrive at happiness through virtue, and in his view the ultimate happiness was to go beyond the cravings of the senses and to be liberated from desires, to rise to the level of the gods and to trust the power of the soul.

With regard to Socrates' methods of instruction, he did not establish a school as such. He had pupils, but they differed in their understanding of his philosophy to the point of contradicting one another; they differed among themselves and with Socrates himself. Three of his followers, however, did establish the most important schools. Firstly, there was the school of Cynicism. Its teachings are consistent with those of Socrates, in that virtue is considered to be knowledge and that one can be instructed in this. Furthermore, this is based upon the elimination of all desires as a means to achieve happiness. To achieve this, some of its proponents advocated seclusion from the world, as well as contempt for its rules and its conventions. One of the most celebrated Cynics was Diogenes. Secondly, there was the Cyrenaic school which was established by Aristippus. According to him, happiness is the goal of existence. He understood happiness as pleasure; thus, everything that leads to pleasure is good. However, to achieve this, man must not give free rein to his appetites; rather, he should exercise self-control. Thirdly, there was the Megarian school. It taught that that which is good is pure being. This school fused Eleatic thought with that of Socrates.

These schools did not bring the philosophy of Socrates to fruition, however. The person who accomplished this, who expanded on Socrates' philosophy and created a comprehensive philosophical system, was Plato. But we shall leave the discussion of his philosophy for another article.

Plato and His Philosophy[1]

Plato was born into an aristocratic family during the period of suffering that ensued following the Peloponnesian wars. He was born in 429 BC – the year in which Pericles died.[2] Like other sons of the nobility, he was given an education. Unusually, however, he did not pursue the same path in life as his aristocratic peers. The political life, with its authority and power, did not appeal to him, nor was he taken in by the pomp of the aristocracy, their titles, and so forth – those things which the young men commonly strove for, especially those of the high-born class. Plato held such things in contempt and, instead, sought the tranquillity of philosophical seclusion. Now, when he reached the age of twenty, he became a companion of Socrates and between them produced something brilliant, as is often the case when a smart, hardworking youth gets together with a great teacher. Plato was not only influenced by Socrates in relation to his views and beliefs, but also in terms of his life and his ethics. It is no secret that Socrates was a good example of a man with a strong will who was capable of controlling his desires; he was someone who lived in accordance with his views and principles and did not deviate from them even when this meant drinking the fatal cup of poison.

---

1 Article from *al-Majalla al-Ma'rifa* November 1931
2 The exact date of Plato's birth is not known with certainty; however, it is generally believed to have been in 428–7 BC, prior to the death of Pericles in 429 BC.

After Socrates died, Plato undertook a number of long journeys during which he visited Megara, Egypt and other places. He derived great benefit from his travels. Furthermore, he acquired knowledge of different peoples and ethics, which brought him enjoyment and delight. Indeed, these travels gave him the opportunity to familiarise himself with both the ancient and newer philosophies, such as Pythagorean philosophy, Megarian philosophy, and others. As we shall see, these philosophies had a profound effect upon his philosophical life. He finally returned to Athens when he was in his forties. There, his pupils gathered around him and he began giving lectures at the Academy. For a long time he lived in a state of tranquillity and contemplation before later setting out on two more journeys which put an end to this peace and reflection. However, he did return to his Academy and resumed his life of thinking and teaching. His serenity was only disturbed in the later years of his life by the division that arose within his school, for which Aristotle is considered to be responsible. Whether Plato was busy with his writing, or whether he was at a wedding banquet – according to various accounts – his spirit passed away gently and calmly as though he were merely drifting into sleep. The philosophy of Plato can be divided into three categories in accordance with the different phases of his life. The first of these phases is the period of his own study, the second is that of his travels, and the third is the period during which he taught.

The Philosophy of the Early Period

During this phase his philosophy was influenced by that of Socrates – an influence which is fully apparent. He was following the path of his teacher in his opposition to the Sophists and in endeavouring to formulate absolute, universal principles with regard to ethics. Plato presents himself to us through the logic of inquiry in his book *Phaedrus*, and if it is true that he wrote this book during his early period, then it is fair to say that he had already reached a high level of conversance with regard to the essence of his ideas – such as his belief concerning the pre-existence of the soul, for example – when he was still but a young man. If we discount *Phaedrus* from our discussion, however, we can more clearly perceive the development of Plato's thought.

Firstly, the dialogues debate the views of Socrates, adopting his manner of inquiry and logic. In Plato's early writings he speaks about certain ethical matters, such as friendship, and the power of endurance. Certain weaknesses and a lack of consistency beset these works, providing a clear indication that they are among the early writings of the philosopher. Secondly, he is distinctly critical of the Sophists, their ideas, and their influence on those around them, through his various responses to them, or through Socrates' opposition to them. He goes on to discuss Socrates' view of virtue as being a type of knowledge that can be taught like other types of knowledge. Thirdly, he opposes the idea held by the Sophists that virtue is based upon subjective perception. In Plato's opinion, virtue is does not have an end other than itself; therefore, that which is good should take the place of pleasure as a moral basis.

The Philosophy of the Middle Period

During this period Plato studied the philosophy of the Eleatics and the Pythagoreans. In this way his own particular philosophy became mature. His studies inspired him to take up the biggest of philosophical questions and prepared him for the liberation of Socratic philosophy from the bonds of working life. His investigation into ethics was not restricted; rather, he gave free rein to his thoughts, which took flight in the spheres of knowledge in search of the principal, objective source of ethics. In this, his thinking had been influenced by the Socratic method which brought structure and universality to his investigation, leading him to reject the Sophist Protagoras who had premised the laws of ethics, among other things, upon the notion of subjectivity. The result of Plato's inquiry was that he arrived at a knowledge of the theory of ideas: he realised that actions are an outcome of knowledge, which in turn is a result of ideas.

The Philosophy of the Late Period

This phase represents the completion of the ethical philosophy of the early period, as well as the profound investigation of issues that took place during the middle period. The outcome of these phases was his creation of a universal, philosophical system that was the first of its kind in the history of human thought. Plato now undertook inquiries of a social nature in which he conceived ideal forms of government and society.

In sum, Plato's philosophy comprised practical sciences as well as theoretical ones. Aristotle's classification of Plato's philosophy – into the categories of natural philosophy, logic, and ethics – is perhaps the most accurate subdivision, insofar as the scope of Plato's inquiries was limited to these three branches of philosophy. In some of his works it can be observed that Plato mixes these branches of philosophy together without any distinction between them. On the other hand, however, *The Republic* is predominantly concerned with ethics, while *Timaeus* is mostly focused upon natural philosophy.

Plato and Protagoras

Protagoras did not differentiate between knowledge and perception. According to him, things are, in reality, what they appear to us to be; perception is above doubt and confusion. And when perceptions differ greatly among individuals – indeed, depending on different circumstances, they can even vary within one individual – then it is illogical to espouse universal principles or general rules. Thus, truths are relative, nothing more. Plato opposed this theory and we shall summarise the proofs for his argument below:

1. If there is no difference between the object and its appearance, or between knowledge and perception, then the perception of any animal, having the power of cognition, can be taken as a true measure of things. Therefore, my own wisdom is true and I am good, in which case there is no benefit to be had from instruction and debate.

2. Belief in this theory involves a rational contradiction, because Protagoras would have to consider any opponent who debates with him, and who accuses him of being in error, as being accurate in both his judgment and perception.

3. This theory requires perception itself, and perception depends upon the subject, i.e., that which is perceptible through the senses. Now, when the subject is unstable, then its constant change will render perception as absurd.

4. Furthermore, Protagoras did not say a word concerning the perception of the intellect. We may hear, see, smell, touch and taste with the senses; however, the integration of these senses, which arise from different organs of the body, takes place in the sphere of our perceptive faculty, not in the senses. We describe things which are perceived through the senses according to their harmony and lack thereof, by their variance or resemblance. We make comparisons between different perceptions, but this is not done by the senses themselves. It is impossible to receive the sensations of hearing through the eye, or of seeing through the ear for that matter.[3]

Just as Plato made a distinction between knowledge and perception, he also drew a line between these and belief; he ranked this as being between knowledge and the absence thereof. The important point here is that Plato did not consider belief to be something confirmed by knowledge.

The Relationship Between Knowledge and Ideas

Existence is comprised of two worlds. There is the visible world, which is constantly advancing, moving from the past toward the future, as it

---

3 Author's own footnote, translated here: 'Some psychologists say that this is not impossible. I recall that in one of William James' books I read his summary of their remarks; they explained that if it is possible to transplant the nerves and capillaries of the eye to the ear, then we would see with our ears.' Mahfouz, Naguib, Ḥawla l-Adab wa-l-Falsafa, Cairo, 2003, p. 38

passes through the present; and there is the world which is always fixed – unchanging, eternal and infinite. We obtain knowledge of the former world through belief and the aid of our senses, but our knowledge of it is confused and disordered. As for the latter world, to gain knowledge of it requires rational thinking and its knowledge is sound and true. Only the logical faculty has the ability to remove the veil from the light of eternal truth hidden behind the external appearances of things. This is true knowledge, and verities were given the designation 'ideas'.

The Theory of the Ideal

Plato constructed the frame of this important philosophical theory using three pillars. The first of these was Socrates' idea concerning universalisation, the second was Heraclitus' notion of changeableness, and the third was the notion of absolute being as envisioned by Parmenides.[4]

Everything in existence – such as the good and the beautiful, strength, man, fire and water, and so on – has its ideal in the world of ideas. It is possible to define this ideal, or idea, as the universal source of variations, with the human being as the universal of an individual person, and the singleness that of the multitude. This is the root of knowledge, its source; it has no relation to experience or the senses. Since everything has an ideal, its existence is neither futile nor accidental; the idea precedes its material reproduction. To better comprehend this we can use the example of the circle. The circle exists in its essence prior to its being drawn. Likewise, all living, physical organisms, their characteristics and relations, have their ideal in the rational world prior to particularities being formed in the material world. Thus, the ideal is the foundation of knowledge and is distinguished by two attributes:

---

4 The original Arabic spelling of this name (برمستيد) is strange enough to warrant a footnote. I believe it is an error in spelling, since it resembles no name that I know. It may be 'Parmenides', as I have written it in the text, but this is not entirely certain. Mahfouz, Naguib, *Hawla l-Adab wa-l-Falsafa*, Cairo, 2003, p. 39

1. The universality of all existing things, which are derived from one type.
2. The ideal exists in and of itself. It is more complete and perfect than the distinctive forms that derive from it. The ideals themselves are ordered according to their degrees of perfection and at the summit is the ideal of the good.

The Relationship Between Ideas and the Realm of Sensation

Plato did not establish this relationship in a manner that is entirely convincing because the evidence which he put forth is disjointed due to inconsistencies. Furthermore, he does not get beyond certain assumptions, nor does he rid us of doubt when he says that phenomena are representations of ideals existing in the realm of ideas. When he discusses the notion of changeableness and investigates its truth, he explains that the eternal core ideas are, alone, the truth. He considers materiality as not having real existence and he views that which is perceived by the senses as being no more than something resembling an existing thing – as something resembling the thing that has true being.

Plato frequently discusses the visible world as though it were a phenomenon which is perceived by the subjective consciousness. Furthermore, in all of his statements, we are given to believe that true being is one, and as for the realm of the senses, it is nothing more than an imperfect copy of this true being. However, it is not long before one encounters significant inconsistency in Plato's investigations which undermines his notion of oneness; namely, he sought to apply this concept of oneness to the soul and the flesh, while at the same time stating that there was perpetual opposition between them. Furthermore, there is inconsistency in his statements concerning materiality and its opposition to the power of eternal ideas. All of this suggests to us that there are two opposing forces, two separate elements, rather than one force, one element.

The Idea of the Good, and the Divine Being

We have learned that ideas in the world of rationality are ordered according to their degrees of perfection, or to put it another way, they are sequential – each one being higher to the one before it. However, this sequence must have an end: there must be a supreme idea that is the source of all ideas. This supreme idea is 'the idea of the good', which is the foundation of knowledge: it is the source of ideals, the starting point of truth, and the fountainhead of rationality. It is above everything and there is no source beyond it, being essential and absolute.

A question that might be asked here is: what is the connection between these ideas and God? I do not have a clear answer to this question. It seems that Plato did not make a particular inquiry into this topic, but the reader of Plato is often convinced that he did not make a distinction between 'the idea of the good' and God.

Nature and How Existence Came to Be

Before existence there was a creative force that acted as a universal, active origin. On one side there was the eternal, ideal world, and on the other there was the darkness which contained within it the origins of the material world. From these two elements the creator made the soul of the world. This is the mystery behind its force, order, and movement. Then, the creative force sent forth the soul of the world to fill the void. It divided the cosmos into two parts which were filled one after the other by the fixed stars and the planets, then the latter part was divided into seven celestial spheres. Next, the four elements came into being and the earth appeared in the void that had been filled by the soul. It is as though the soul of the world were the medium between the world of ideas and the world of objects – the medium upon which virtue relied in the making of matter.

The Soul

The soul is eternal, and among its most important characteristics is the aspiration for knowledge of the eternal deity and other fundamental concepts, through contemplation of the world of ideals. However, its connectedness with the flesh is no less important than its connectedness with the world of ideas.[5] During the soul's union with the flesh it is subject to the same movements and changes which the body is subject to. It is also affected by its sensual urges, its desires and its vices. From this stems the struggle between our higher and lower natures. Each tries to gain mastery and bring the other over to its side through force and violence. The influence is not purely that of the body on the soul; rather, they affect each other mutually. The soul tries to extricate the body from its entanglement so that it will transcend sensual desires. In the soul there is an eternal aspect which belongs to rationality, as well as an aspect which has no connection with rationality and which is subject to transition. It is between these two aspects of the soul that the quality of courage is generated, and since this quality can be found in children and some animals, it is not related to rationality in any way. Generally, we can discern three distinct aspects of the soul: the rational soul which resides in the head, the spirited soul residing in the heart, and the appetitive soul in the stomach. The punishment for souls that are governed by the desires of the senses is that they are reincarnated once, or several times, in other bodies – base ones, perhaps – until such a time as they are cleansed of their impurities.

Ethics

Ethics can be summarised as the knowledge of intention and outcome. Ethics is the theory of ideals in practical form. It speaks of the exalted good, or the absolute good, which, in Plato's view, is the summit of truth and the greatest ideal. As for the soul, its aim is extrication from the bonds of sensual appetites and desires in order to become pure and upright, and ascend to the level of the gods. This, however, can

---

5 Mahfouz uses the term *bi-l-mala'i l-a'lā* which means 'with the angels' or 'with the heavenly host'. Since this would seem to be anachronistic, I have translated it as 'with the world of ideas'. Mahfouz, Naguib, *Hawla l-Adab wa-l-Falsafa*, Cairo, 2003, p. 42

only be attained by mastering the self, by abstaining from vice, through the tranquillity of thinking and contemplation, and through immersion in the knowledge of truth – in short, by applying oneself to philosophy.

Concerning Plato's opinion on virtue, he embraced Socrates' view that it is a type of knowledge that can be taught like other types of knowledge. He considered virtue to be both one and many at the same: one insofar as each virtue can be considered to possess the properties of 'absolute virtue', and many in relation to the numerous peculiarities which are represented in each. As for the most important of the fundamental virtues, he categorised these in light of his previous division concerning the soul: the virtue of the rational mind is wisdom, the virtue of the heart is courage, and moderation is the virtue of the senses, to which he then added uprightness.

Plato's Republic

Plato's republic is a city-state constructed in his imagination. He conceived it as one which would provide for the prosperity of its citizens – these would be few in number so that it would be possible for them to be acquainted with one another – and in which everything would serve the common good. To this end the city-state would exercise complete authority over its individual citizens, their work, their social class, their sexual relations and progeny – and possessions would be common property – as though they were children who know neither a mother nor a father and have only their city-state, for the sake of which they must sacrifice everything.

His republic would have three social classes: the guardians, the warriors, and the farmers. They would work together for the state like the organs of one body, with each class performing its own particular function. Just as the health of the body can only ensured by the division of labour among its organs, likewise, the prosperity of the state could only be ensured by each of the three classes performing those duties for which they are responsible. Here we can observe that this tripartite division of social class follows from Plato's aforementioned division of the soul's aspects. Ownership and marriage would be permitted to members of the farmer class but forbidden to members of the other two classes. Perhaps the reason for this due to the great importance which Plato attached to these two classes: one would establish the community's constitution, guarantee its freedom, and strive on its behalf to find the best means for its prosperity, while the other would provide for the community's defence, and protect it from enemies that would bring harm and ruin. The classes, however, were not conceived of as rigid. If a child from a lower class was found to be intelligent, he or she would be raised to be a guardian, for example. Those with disabilities, however, were to be killed regardless of what class they belonged to.

At this point we shall conclude our discussion of Plato's philosophy. If I wished to give a full summary and commentary of it, as is its due, a large tome would not suffice to contain it.

Anton Chekhov (The Russian Author)[1]

Anton Chekhov was born on the 19 of January 1860 in the city of Taganrog.[2] The family he was born into were poor and of no historical note. Chekhov's grandfather had worked as a serf for a wealthy lord but later purchased his freedom from earnings that he had put by. He raised his son (Anton's father) to be thrifty and careful with money, and in a short space of time he was able to progress from being a lowly clerk to being the owner of a shop and the pillar of a family composed of four brothers and one sister.[3] The family was extremely conservative and strictly observed religious traditions. The children received a religious education from their mother and father, at home and at the church. The father's passion for church music was such that he made all of his children join the choir. Their young voices would join with the other voices of the choir as they sang hymns. However, despite the painstaking efforts that were made to ensure that they had a religious upbringing, the outcome was the opposite of what their father had intended. As a mature man, Anton later wrote that, 'When I recall the memories of my childhood, it seems dreadful in my mind. I have no religion now. When I and my brothers used to sing in the church the audience would

---

1 Article from *al-Siyasa al-Usbu'iya* 8 May 1933
2 This is an error in the original text. Chekhov was actually born on the 29 January 1860.
3 Mahfouz seems to be referring to Anton Chekhov's father who at one time owned a grocery shop. He fathered one daughter and five sons, one of whom was Anton.

look at us admiringly, envying our parents, but the sense of degradation we felt inside harmed us – we were like little slaves aboard a galley.' This upbringing was not fruitless however, because the beautiful hymns carved an indelible mark on the soul of Chekhov and imbued his heart with a love for them: it was this that led to the young Chekhov to incline toward, and be interested in, the Russian language.

When he got a little older he attended a parochial school where he had to endure a teacher who was stern and cruel, yet lacking in knowledge and intelligence. In this way he missed out on what should have been a happy period of his life and would later associate it in his memory with barrenness and privation. It is for this reason that he would always say that he never had a childhood.

Later, Chekhov attended grammar school. Here, he was initially thought to be lazy and stupid but he was well-liked because he was not competitive and always had a charming smile on his lips. However, towards the end of his time at this school he became completely transformed: his indifference ceased, he shook off laziness, focused his mind, foolishness vanished from him, and the life-blood of vitality pulsed through his veins. Although this change dampened his sense of humour, nevertheless, he remained cheerful, reading novels aloud to make others laugh; he would impersonate different voices and alter the appearance of his face until he was no longer recognisable. His brothers and anyone who witnessed this would be astonished, and delighted, by it.

After attending grammar school, he went to a school of medicine. His father had gone bankrupt by this time, and facing destitution he was forced to work as a simple clerk. However, it was not enough to support the family and Anton too was forced to work in order to save the family from starving to death. This truly was one of the most difficult periods that this author suffered during his life: he was a medical student – and we all know the arduous work involved in studying medicine – and at the same time a writer composing stories to entertain readers after dinner. We can imagine the suffering of a writer when, rather than writing from inspiration and enjoyment, he has to write in order to earn his living and keep the wolf from the door. On top of this he was living in a poor neighbourhood where the din of children mingled with the shouts of adolescent boys. This kind of life would have been like a living hell because one cannot taste the beauty of existence, and experience life, unless one can pause for a little while to contemplate it and to enjoy it. He knew that his writing was poor; he had tried to write as he wanted and pleased, but he was not given much encouragement in this.

Eventually, life granted him relief from some of its burdens. He graduated from medical school and entered a hospital to gain practical training. For the first time he was given a chance to experience one of life's pleasures: living in the countryside. Here he mixed with many rural peasants and people of office which would come to have a profound effect on his imagination. Later, the head of the newspaper *Novoye Vremya* asked Chekhov to write respectable stories for him; perhaps he was very happy that he no longer had to write frivolous tales, for he applied himself to this work with enthusiasm and caught the attention of some of the greatest litterateurs. Even Dmitry Grigorovich wrote to him saying, 'You have a real talent, a talent which exalts you above the modern writers of your generation.' Though his aim had previously been to earn money, he now strove for the sake of artistic excellence until he won the Pushkin Prize and his fame spread. But the constant exertion and continual work took a bad toll upon his health and exhausted his strength; he began to show the symptoms of tuberculosis. Yet, he concealed the illness, taking care to suppress its symptoms in his chest so that his mother would not find out: he feared the pain and sadness it would cause her if she knew. Neither his illness, nor anything else, would prevent him from continuing his work, however. He wrote successful plays for the theatre such as *Ivanov* and *Uncle Vanya*. When one of his plays flopped he felt discouraged for a time about writing for the theatre. Had this play not been restaged in Moscow, where it was a resounding success, then the theatre might have been deprived of Chekhov's pen.

The horizons of Chekhov's life expanded; it swelled with experience and a true understanding of things. His financial circumstances improved and he moved to Moscow, but his illness worsened severely, to the extent that he could no longer hide it, and those whom he feared would find out about it, did. With a heavy heart he was forced into exile from his beloved homeland, going to the south of France. For a time he remained there, enduring the pains of the illness and nursing an ardent longing for Moscow and its inhabitants. When he felt an improvement in his health he hastened to return to his homeland. Chekhov knew an actress called Olga Leonardovna Knipper and for the first time we see his life tinted with that beautiful rose colour of love, which brought their hearts together. They married and travelled together, each delighting in love. But the illness returned to haunt him and deprived him of tranquillity; he went back into his exile, leaving his wife, who returned to Moscow in order to pursue her career. One can imagine the state he was in, afflicted in both his heart and chest, and far from his homeland.

The severity of the illness intensified and he travelled to Germany accompanied by his wife. She relates to us the pains that her husband suffered, but she also draws particular attention to the enduring cheerfulness of his spirit which retained its good humour and playfulness; indeed, he continued to make her laugh despite the fact that she was very worried for him. In the end, that strong, rustic body was vanquished in the face of the malignant illness and the author passed away.

Something in Chekhov's nature prevented him from giving a clear illustration of his own character. He did not leave behind personal memoirs which would be of use to the historian. The fact is that his many letters and the like mostly deal with general literary and philosophical topics. Thus, the only reliable sources for those who wish to gain an insight into this literary soul are his works themselves and some of his private letters. It is right that we should speak about his faith, for the faith of the man, or his lack thereof, is the most accurate measure by which to weigh his deeds and actions – and Chekhov had clearly stated that he had lost faith in Christianity when he was a child. His taste for religious freedom endured and he continued to enjoy himself, fool around, and work without disturbing the happiness of his heart with pressing questions of faith which might induce a measure of pain. In his later work, however, one senses a gravity in his writing; it is as though his view of life underwent a transformation, as though life, in his view, had grown in significance, and his questions about life and death were advancing to the point where they almost touched the bitterness which filled his delicate soul. He emerged from the tower of his mind to encounter the many social problems of the time and a deep concern about them took hold of him. This concern induced him to expose himself to the trepidations of travelling, just to find out about new people and new ideas. This concern of his can clearly be seen in the incident involving his resignation from the Academy of Sciences in protest after Maxim Gorky's election to it had been rejected on account of his political views. Chekhov, like other Russian writers, was concerned about issues of labour. Here I will quote one of his remarks so that we can gain an insight into his reformist vision: 'If we all – whether those of us who inhabit the cities or those who live in the countryside – agreed to divide up amongst ourselves the labour that we carry out to satisfy our physical needs, then none of us would need to work more than two or three hours each day. For the remainder of the day we would be at leisure; we would dedicate this time to the arts and sciences, all of us would spend it searching for truth and the meaning of life. I'm certain that the face of truth would be revealed to us. Man would be able to free himself from the constant fear of death which burns him in a fire of torment.' In the end Chekhov was guided to faith – a faith in humanity, its future and its progress. To get a sense of this faith of his you need only read one of his works and you are sure to perceive it if you read the text closely.

The reality of human lives aroused both indignation and compassion in Chekhov. He continually portrayed the wretched conditions of human beings, and he accused this of being the cause for all of the suffering which besets man, including those tendencies toward enmity, hatred, selfishness, and wickedness, which fill his soul. When you read one of Chekhov's works you might imagine that you are reading *Heartbreak House* by George Bernard Shaw,[4] if you pay attention the

---

4 George Bernard Shaw adapted the style of Chekhov for his play *Heartbreak House: A Fantasia in the Russian Manner on English Themes*, which was published in 1919.

theme and the direction of the plot, for he conceives the world, or Europe, through a family in which each of the members are stricken by something that causes them to stray from the path of happiness. Then, towards the end of the work there is a pleasant appeal for happiness and a clear optimism for a blissful future.

Yet, in the midst of these social movements and human difficulties Chekhov remained an artist who was true to art. On this he has stated, 'Bias has its roots in man's inability to rise above the trivialities of things. The artist should endeavour to be an impartial witness – no more than that. I am not a liberal, I am not a conservative, and I am not a reformist. I like being an artist, nothing more.'

Three of Our Writers[1]

Our literary Nahda is about to bid the period of transition farewell in order to usher in a new era that has strong foundations and clear goals.[2] This momentous work – that of guiding the transition – has been undertaken by a number of great writers who continue to nourish our literature with impassioned outpourings from their sublime spirits. If I desired to present each one here and give them their due, then this article would never end. I do, however, wish to discuss three of them, three writers who can be seen to be representatives of our Nahda in its various aspects. I am not talking about them as critics or as historians, but as readers who have had a connection with one another over a long period of time, and who have greatly influenced each other. These three are: Abbas el-Akkad, Taha Hussein, and Salama Moussa.

Abbas el-Akkad

El-Akkad is a creature of instinct. By this I mean that his intuition is discerning, his perception true, and his character unimpaired – that

1 Article from *al-Majalla al-Ma'rifa* February 1934
2 The Nahda (*al-nahḍa*) means 'the awakening' and refers to a cultural renaissance that occurred in the late 19th century and early 20th century in the Middle East. The movement was greatly influenced by contact with the West and is seen as a period of modernisation and reform. Egypt is one of the countries seen as having made important contributions to the Nahda; indeed, Mahfouz seems to be referring in this article the literary Nahda of Egypt insofar as the writers he discusses here are Egyptian.

is, he possesses a natural talent for getting to the facts of a matter and discovering its essence. This is a level of perfection which the Sufi attains through much exertion, and which the artist possesses in his nature and character.[3] If you wish to verify what I say then simply read the poetry of el-Akkad.

In my opinion el-Akkad is, above all, a brilliant poet. Among the most distinguishing features of his work is the absence of superficial embellishments and melodic expression; however, there is a depth of signification which you can feel and taste. You can discover an animated spirit that seems to move and change whenever you examine his work closely. Such things belong to the soul, whose gate reason and intelligence are incapable of forcing open – only the delicate, sensitive perception may pass through it and glean the life and mystery therein.

El-Akkad's common sense is apparent in the way in which he calls for the renewal of poetry and literature. While we may understand 'renewal' in the conventional sense, as the call for a new doctrine to replace an old one – such as the call for realism, or idealism, and so forth – el-Akkad views renewal differently. He never advocates for any specific doctrine in particular; rather, he revolts against the blind imitation and conformity he sees in others, and calls for the liberation of consciousness and rationality. He challenges us to comprehend with our minds and to perceive with our consciousnesses. Such a principle is in opposition to giving support for any one particular doctrine or other, because the call for a particular doctrine is, itself, a form of imitation. Thus, if you were to blindly follow el-Akkad, you would not be one of his true followers! His view makes life out of art, which, just like this life, is always changing, being renewed, and constantly moving forward.

Through literature, el-Akkad is exalted to the apex of perfection and veneration. This is only natural, because the gift he possesses is that of the Sufi, and how can one ask a Sufi to not venerate his Beloved who reveals the hidden mysteries to him?

---

3 A Sufi (ṣūfī) is an adherent of Islamic mysticism.

Taha Hussein

As for Taha, he is a man of intelligence and this shines through in two important ways: through simplicity and irony. Indeed, when you read Taha Hussein you will not come across an unusual word, a complicated sentence, an awkward expression, or an abstruse concept; you will understand everything as he intends you to, and you will be pleased and happy, stimulated and enlightened. This simplicity, however, does not indicate that the subject being dealt with by the author is itself simple, or banal. Rather, it is more a sign of the penetrating intelligence behind it, a mathematical intelligence – or a French intelligence, if you like – which does not tolerate abstruseness or complexity, and which presents its conclusion in the simplicity of a mathematical axiom even if the subject is very difficult to digest and articulate. This is a simplicity which is truly inimitable.

As for Taha's sense of irony, this comes across very clearly in his style and the way in which he depicts things. It is, in its essence, the bringing together of contradictory elements through the use of indirect allusion and intimation, and it is sustained by a capacity for relentless observation and circumspection. Intelligence leads to scepticism, and scepticism has been the basis for Taha Hussein's investigations. His valuable research, which has become a model for intellectuals, has had a significant impact in renewing interest in Islamic literary works.

Salama Moussa

Salama Moussa is distinguished by his practical thinking. He pays little regard to theories, nor does he rely on abstract thinking or artistic contemplation. He is only concerned with theory insofar as it can be practically applied; this is because his interest lies in life and in perfection in this life. You cannot mention Mr Moussa without also mentioning Darwin and his theory of evolution. This theory has had a profound influence on Moussa and represents the source of his highest ideals for mankind and social life. His foremost preoccupation is social reform: he has completed extensive tours and made great sacrifices in order to promote the modernisation of religion, the emancipation of women, and advancement for the peasant and the worker. He was the first to appeal for economic nationalism and his call had a considerable impact on the minds of young people; we can see that it has strong, vigorous support, which is growing day by day. On the whole, he is a great literary innovator. He does not view literature as an end in and of itself, however; rather, he sees it as a means to achieve reform and progress in society, and in life generally. Moussa relies more on psychology as a means of appealing to people than on the use of logic and argument. He conveys what he wants to say in brief, clear statements, which he repeats with frequency until they have taken root in the mind as one of its guiding elements. Thus, his principles become firmly established in people's minds, influencing his enemies before even his own supporters.

I have written here about the distinguishing characteristics of each of these writers, but I would not like it to be thought that this is all there is to them; no, these are only those traits of character which are distinctive in each. Would anyone deny that the treatises of el-Akkad are models of forward thinking and intellectual genius? Would anyone deny that Taha Hussein has produced literary works which attain the absolute heights of beauty and eloquence? And would any reader deny that Salama Moussa has written articles and books of criticism which rank as the best of what has been written on the subjects they deal with?

Now, if I wished to analyse and categorise them – as is the natural inclination of the mind – then it would be true to say that el-Akkad is the spirit of the literary Nahda, Taha Hussein is its rational mind, and Salama Moussa is its will.

Love and the Sexual Impulse[1]

I am neither joking nor exaggerating when I say that the role that love plays in our physical and social lives is more important, and of greater consequence, than any other factor. Indeed, it is almost as though it lies hidden behind every action, just as the breath of life lies concealed in each living organ, driving it and directing it. Perhaps you already know that there are scientists who attribute to it every activity in the life of the human being without exception. I always try to steer clear of general, universal principles, however; they provoke apprehension and doubt in me. Therefore, let us content ourselves by simply acknowledging that love occupies an important place in the life of the individual and in society.

It should be mentioned that some of the philosophers conceived of love's influence as not being restricted to the lives of humans and animals only, but as extending to the natural world itself – to the life of matter, or, more accurately, to the being of matter. These philosophers viewed it as one of the constituent elements of being. The ancient philosopher Empedocles stated that the four known elements are the source of existence and that everything which occurs is a result of their combining or separating.[2] According to him, this combination or separation of elements occurs due to the agency of two forces: love and hatred. Furthermore, Arthur Schopenhauer claimed that egoism exists

---

1 Article from *al-Majalla al-Jadida* March 1934
2 The 'four known elements' being referred to here are the classical elements: earth, water, air, and fire.

in the elements of nature, taking the forms of repulsion and attraction, or hatred and love. It is, without doubt, a wonderful thing that man would uncover the essence of this beautiful mystery, this irresistible force which controls our lives, which directs our minds, and which affects the greatest impact on our present and future states.

The topic of love is closely linked to that of the sexual impulse. No matter how lofty an amorous affection may be, the bond connecting it to its source – the basic instinct in man's nature – cannot be severed. Indeed, if this connection were to be severed, then perhaps it would put an end to that affection and its loftiness both. In order to understand what love is, we must first concern ourselves with understanding this impulse. The following words are applicable to it:

> The sexual impulse is based upon secretions produced by special glands which control the growth of the genitals. This impulse is common among all living creatures, but its condition varies. This indicates that it is subject to general evolution, because the degree of this impulse varies from the simple organisms to the large animals and again in the higher animals.

Professor Théodule-Armand Ribot has stated that the sex impulse in its simplistic form, as found in microscopic creatures, reveals its vital, organic properties. Among infusoria, a pair will come into contact and join with one another, becoming as one. Through this process the life in each of them is strengthened and they multiply, then they separate from one another, each having endowed the other with a new vitality which enables it to divide and multiply itself – a process that continues for a long time until the organism dwindles away. This process is reminiscent of what happens to cells in the human body, how they divide and separate. Some physiologists ascribe to infusoria a consciousness which experiences pleasure in sexual sensation. They say that before one of them connects with another it feels a mysterious desire to join and mate, and that this desire is what attracts it to the other. However, in the joining and dividing of infusoria others see only chemical interactions devoid of life and consciousness. Opinions such

as this, however, because of their radicalism, are not viewed as commendable when it comes to the study of psychological phenomena.
Thus, some psychologists, such as Dimas,[3] are reluctant to formulate
any relationship between bodily cells and physiological, psychological
phenomena where the sexual impulse is not taken into account when
studying these chemical, biological interactions.

In the higher creatures the sexual impulse takes the form of a desire,
of a pressing need. Its strength or feebleness does not affect the will of
the individual, nor does the individual's will and desire determine its
strength or feebleness. Some doctors and physiologists go so far as to
believe that all need is psychological, but that it is caused by the growth
of the genitals and the glands which are connected to them. This is
the opinion of the materialists; they consider psychological states, or
mental phenomena, as being effects which have been produced by the
physical body as it has become increasingly complex over the course
of its evolution. Krafft-Ebing has stated that, 'Sexuality emerges when
it does due to sensations coming from the external sexual organs as
they develop.' Furthermore, Henri-Étienne Beaunis has said that these
organs suddenly produce new sensations, the effects of which spread
throughout the nervous system. In this way the subject's intelligence,
feelings and morals are altered.

There are other scientists, however, such as Joanny Roux, who reject
these views. They assert that the sexual impulse is independent of
the genitals and the sensation which they produce – even if they do
acknowledge the huge importance of these inner sensations in the
development of the sex impulse. Roux views this impulse as having
two states. The first of these is a latent, general desire that lies hidden
throughout the nervous system. When the human subject experiences
the force of this desire he feels the need to gratify it but does not know
how to do this. Rousseau described this psychological state brilliantly
when he said, 'Straight after I would weep and sigh, I would become

---

3 It is unclear to me to whom d-y/ī-m-ā-s (ديماس) refers. Not untypically, Mahfouz
provides no forename. I have taken the liberty of using 'Dimas' in the text.
Mahfouz, Naguib, Ḥawla l-Adab wa-l-Falsafa, Cairo, 2003, p. 61

agitated and confused. I would long for a joy about which I knew nothing; yet, despite having no notion of what this should be, I felt my deprivation of it.' The second of these states is where desire is clear, fixed in place, and the object of its gratification is known. This is how it is seen by scientists who believe in the independence of psychological life without denying that there is a strong relationship, and mutual interaction, between it and physical being.

No matter how greatly views on this impulse differ, and no matter how numerous the doctrines which try to determine its origin, nevertheless, there is no doubt concerning its existence. It is strong, established, and extends its power over the life of both the individual and the collective. My discussion of it – from the naturalist, physiological viewpoint – in no way deals with the full spectrum of opinions on the subject, but the intention of this is not to present everything that can be said on it. Admittedly, if this essay were to be compared with the many other studies which address the topic from different viewpoints which elucidate the effect of this impulse on the life of the individual and society, if it were to be compared with all of these, then perhaps it would be found to be mediocre and simplistic. I am of the opinion that society facilitates all of the complex outcomes that result from it, and all of the roles which it plays. The physical actuality of society exerts an influence over the lives of individuals that is without equal. It is society, with its laws and customs, that produces all of the situations and outward forms which clothe this impulse, but which also signify its presence. Society is the natural stage whereon it acts out its roles: godliness and evil, obedience and defiance, submission and revolt, exaltation and decadence. The explanation for this, in my opinion, is that society, through its conditions and circumstances, both wages war against the sexual impulse and protects it, subdues it and empowers it, it channels it and provides it with that which will awaken it and invigorate it. Society suppresses the sexual impulse and fights against it by means of its religion, tradition, and laws. Perhaps society is severe, for it renounces the impulse, and thinks little of dressing it in sullied robe of shame and disgrace. On the other hand, however, through society's observer, through its dancer, though its arts and literature – and, indeed, by society's prohibition itself – it strengthens and awakens the sexual impulse. It is almost as if society causes both its strength and weakness, and its life or death. Naturally, this produces a state of conflict; we can witness in society the conditions for immoderation and excessiveness, wherein shots are exchanged between the monastic cells and the abodes of licentiousness. There are those among us who are exalted to the heavens by this impulse, there are those who sink to the depths on account of it, and there are those who waver between the two in a state of agitation and misery.

In any case, I do not have the time to provide a detailed discussion of these states; rather, by discussing this impulse, I merely wanted to pave the way for a discussion on love.

Philosophy According to the Philosophers[1]

The importance of philosophy has become the topic of a protracted dispute in recent times. Many now regard it as a remnant of the past that no longer has any place among the modern sciences, which accomplish its purpose perfectly and whose findings can be empirically verified. The debate over philosophy, however, is not purely about whether there is an abundance of reasons for its existence or if there is an absence thereof. An important element of the debate involves the definition of its subject and the comprehension of its meaning. Étienne Geoffroy Saint-Hilaire has stated that philosophy is a branch of knowledge whose subject matter was never strictly defined. This may be true if we consider it in terms of subject matter, but what is the value of such a consideration? Does the subject matter determine the philosophy? Or is it that there is an idea, or an intellectual precept, latent in the various forms, whose clarity and distinctness generally follow the progress of science? In order to define the meaning of philosophy and, thereby, determine its value, we should first acquaint ourselves with the views of the philosophers on philosophy.

There is no mention of philosophy in the poetical works of Homer or of Hesiod. At first its meaning is general and imprecise, signifying inquisitiveness and intellection of any kind. We first encounter the word in the writings of Herodotus when Croesus says to Solon, 'What I meant was that you have travelled in many of lands, observing

---

1 Article from *al-Majalla al-Jadida* January 1935

them and philosophising', and in the words of Pericles as recorded by Thucydides, 'We love beauty to a degree and we philosophise without caution.' Thucydides believed that he was conversant in philosophy because he had accrued many collections of poetry and sophistry. Pythagoras was, in fact, the first person to attempt a definition of philosophy. It was he who said that only God possesses wisdom in abundance, but that it is sufficient for man to have a love for it and to pursue it in order to attain the rank of perfection. The term 'philosopher' did not become current, however, until the time of Socrates. Prior to this, philosophers were referred to as 'sages', 'naturalists', or 'Sophists'.

Among the first philosophers philosophy encompassed intellection, or the interpretation of things, and wisdom, or the practice of virtue. Their wisdom was practical and their intellection was applied to the external world. They were the heirs of the poets who tried to explicate knowledge, being, and the source of its creation, using a theological method predicated on the historical account of the gods. For their part, they tried to answer the question of the source of existence and the origin of man, and they attempted to gain knowledge of this source. At one time they claimed that its source was the elements, at another time they said that it was atoms, and on yet another occasion that it was numbers. This is an understanding of philosophy which qualifies it as a general and comprehensive science of all human knowledge.

When Socrates came along he changed the focus of intellection from nature to man. For this reason Cicero said of Socrates that he had caused philosophy to descend from the heavens to the earth, and that he had introduced it to the cities and homes, be it politics or ethics. Socrates is not only considered to be the founder of ethics, as a branch of philosophy, indeed, the principle of his logic remained the basis of human psychology for twenty centuries. To this philosopher, the subject of science was that which is constant in things whose particulars and non-essential characteristics vary, or, to put it another way, the aim of science is to determine the basic essence which forms the substance of a thing. The logic of Socrates was further developed by Plato and ended up with Aristotle's syllogism which came to dominate world thinking throughout classical antiquity and the Middle Ages, right up until the time of René Descartes.

Plato restored to philosophy its universality. It did not revert to being simply the science of ethics or of nature, nor did it revert to representing the sciences as a whole; rather, it came to be seen as the supreme science which extended its authority over all sciences. The subject of science was not that which is perceived by the senses, which was seen as variable and as containing no truth, nor was it intuitive thought which arrives at truth by means of a lucky inspiration but which does not have the weight of proof behind it. No, for Plato, the subject of science was the eternal essence which constitutes the truth of a thing. This subject is 'the idea', or *l'idée*, which is the source of every truth both in the rational mind and in existence. Ideas are the eternal models of all things. To Plato, philosophy had a significance beyond the sciences, and nature was that which is known through metaphysics – though he did not use the term 'metaphysics'.

Aristotle employed philosophy in its comprehensive sense, signifying all scientific inquiry. To him it was a general science comprised of three categories: contemplative science, practical science, and poetic science. The subjects of both the poetic and contemplative sciences are susceptible to change and alteration. As for the subject of practical science, it exists in its own right independently of the human will. Aristotle employed the word 'philosophy' to signify the different sciences; however, he viewed being as philosophy's principal subject – that is, the essence of being. From this arises the search for primary causes. Concerning philosophy, Aristotle attributed to it the following characteristics:

1. It comprises everything pertaining to human capacity.
2. It attains distinction through impartiality and sublime contemplation.
3. It is free from every goal except attainment of knowledge.
4. It has a sacred character because it is preoccupied with divine matters.

With regard to the Stoics, they fashioned a philosophy that better resonated with the mentality of the general populace. For the Stoics, wisdom was the intellection of both divine matters as well as human ones. Like Socrates, they tended towards practicality and morality in their philosophy. Contemplation was a cornerstone on which they built their moral principles. Furthermore, they believed in the concept of philosophical oneness and they expressed this through the use of analogy. For example, they said that philosophy is like an animal whose sinews are logic, whose flesh is ethics, and whose nature is the soul. Epicureanism accords with Stoicism in its desire for practicality in philosophy. Epicurus viewed philosophy as a practical science for the achievement of a happy life. He did not deny that there were distinctions between the various sciences, such as natural science, logic, and ethics; however, he considered ethics to be the supreme science to which all other sciences lead.

When East and West came together in Alexandria a new kind of philosophy came into being: mystical philosophy.[2] Philo began to harmonise Greek philosophy and the teachings of the Jewish religion. Plotinus, on the other hand, modified the philosophy of Plato to create Neo-Platonism. He called for the annihilation of the self in God, and in this way he transformed the original philosophical character of Platonism.[3] He mingled science with myths and, by doing so, philosophy lost precision in its meaning.

Having discussed all of the above, is it still possible to comprehend philosophy as having a precise meaning among the Greeks? The truth is that Greeks did not define philosophy in a manner that precisely

---

2 The term used here is al-ṣūfīya, which means 'mysticism', generally, but more specifically refers to 'Sufism'. Mahfouz may be addressing the link between Neo-Platonism, with its more mystical elements, and Islamic mysticism which came later but was influenced by the former.

3 Mahfouz uses the Sufi term al-fanāʾ here, meaning 'annihilation of the self (in God)'. This is probably an outcome of the translation of Neo-Platonic works in which Arabic terminologies were adopted to signify Greek philosophical terms, in this case henosis.

detailed what it signified and what it did not signify. However, this does not prevent anyone from learning about some of the elements which have been incorporated into the body of philosophy by those philosophers from whom they originated. Thus, the philosopher does not study the lesser sciences merely for the sake of it; rather, he does so as a means to construct his philosophy. In this sense philosophy is the philosopher's attempt to gain knowledge of existence and man, the attempt to construct general principles and apply them to everything. Philosophy, therefore, is not a lesser science, nor is it an aggregate of sciences – it is a universal science for the study of existence on the basis that it is a single totality.

During the early Christian era philosophy was employed in the formulation of religious doctrine, and when the Middle Ages arrived the concern of thinkers was confined to reconciling philosophy with the new religion which swept away everything in its path. At that time the aspiration of these philosophers was to utilise philosophy in order to elucidate nature, man, and the soul, while taking great care not to contradict religion in any way. Saint Anselm of Canterbury, who was a follower of Plato, said, 'I believe, so that I will understand'. This statement clearly indicates that faith represented the basis of clear understanding. Another saint, Thomas Aquinas, however, made a distinction between the sphere of reason and that of faith. According to him, reason might lead to faith, but religious truths cannot be proven through use of reason, and that to conclude otherwise would represent a gross transgression against the sanctity of faith. The curious philosophical questions during those times were concerned with faith and religious matters. As for the philosophical problems of classical philosophers, scholars now worked to reconcile these with the Christianity.

When the Renaissance arrived it rose up against both the ancient methods of philosophy as well as the newer ones from the Middle Ages. Two principal voices loudly called for the independence of philosophy: those of Sir Francis Bacon and Descartes. The matter of faith, with the many problems surrounding it, and philosophy, with its own abstruse subjects, could not be reconciled with one another. Bacon divided human knowledge into the categories of history, poetry, and

philosophy, in the manner of his division of the soul into the three categories of memory, imagination, and reason. By this it can be understood that everything which is the subject of reason is philosophy,
because philosophy includes all varieties of the sciences. However,
the principal philosophy, in particular, must be differentiated – this is
the general science. It consists of all of the sciences, which are as the
branches to the tree's trunk. The subject of the principal philosophy is,
firstly, the common principles shared by all the sciences, and secondly,
the general laws of the universe. Bacon divided science into three
categories:

1. The science of God, which comprises natural theology.
2. Angelology.
3. The science of the being, which itself has two branches: the
   theoretical and the practical. The theoretical branch comprises
   natural science, which investigates the efficient cause and the
   material cause, and metaphysics which investigates the formal
   cause and final cause. The practical branch, on the other hand,
   comprises alchemy and mechanics.

Descartes' view of philosophy differs little from that of Bacon's;
however, his view has greater clarity and definition. To Descartes, philosophy is the universal science. It is not the sciences as an aggregate,
but the science of rational principles. Furthermore, it is both theoretical and practical; the practical aspect, however, is entirely dependent
upon the theoretical – which is reminiscent of what has been said by
Epicurus – and its subjects comprise God, nature, and man. Descartes
conceived of it as a mathematical science in its method of investigation. It is based upon principles and makes deductions by use of
analogy.

These principles are known to us by virtue of simple reason; uncer-
tainty does not enter into it, nor are they subject to becoming entangled. God's being ensures their silence, but by them the philosopher
is able to deduce all of the truths which pertain to God, man, and
nature. If you cast your eye over what I have presented concerning

the characteristics of modern philosophy which arose following the Renaissance, and what I have put forth concerning the characteristics of the older philosophies which preceded it, then you will certainly find a perfect resemblance between them in terms of both form and construction. The subjects which Plato and Aristotle were preoccupied with investigating are the same as those which concerned Descartes. Yet, is there an element which distinguishes the philosophy of the latter from his classical predecessors?

The fact of the matter is that philosophy is the spirit of investigation. It clearly underwent a process of change but its sphere of activity was preserved. The ancient philosophers would contemplate existence and receive the ideas that were revealed to him without having a doubt as to their value. There was a general faith in reason and the human soul that only the most exceptional among the Greek philosophers deviated from. Descartes, however, directed philosophy in a new direction because he had doubts about both rationality and the soul, and misgivings about the apparatus of knowledge. Inevitably, therefore, he was sceptical about knowledge itself.

What is it that proves that the rational mind is a suitable instrument for attaining knowledge? How are we to be assured that the mind can discern things as they really are? Is it inconceivable that it could be at fault, and not the senses? Whenever we view something the perceptive faculty intervenes to convince us that what we see is just as it is. Subsequently, however, if it happens that we alter the position from which we view the thing, moving back and forth, for example, then our impressions of it will change insofar as we encounter it from different viewpoints. Despite this, however, we still persist in discovering the truth of something with the aid of rationality. Is it so inconceivable that the rational mind could err and go astray? Is it inconceivable that there are exalted minds that understand things truly, in ways that we cannot? What is it that makes us put our trust in our minds? What is it that makes us all believe in learning? Philosophy tends toward critique. It critiques the human soul so that its worth can be judged and that its power to be an instrument of perception can be verified. When Descartes arrived at this truth, he became convinced of both his soul and of science. It was on this basis that he philosophised.

Descartes paved the way for the philosophers who followed after him. They, however, did not uphold philosophy's universality as he had; strong efforts were made to turn philosophy into a science that would be separate from the other sciences – one which had its own particular subject matter and intellectual boundaries. To John Locke philosophy represented the study of the human mind, to George Berkeley and David Hume it was the study of human nature, and to Étienne Bonnot de Condillac it was the analysis of the senses. In other words, the subject of philosophy came to be confined to the examination of the psyche and its phenomena, whereas before its essential purpose had been to gain knowledge of the origins of things and the universe. The emergence of this new direction is considered to be a great development in the history of philosophy, and when Immanuel Kant came along he added to it with a new and comprehensive critique that was no less momentous than what had preceded him, but I shall leave the discussion of this for another time.

What Is the Meaning of Philosophy?[1]

Generally, philosophy was a comprehensive science that was not strictly defined – a science of everything so to speak. More precisely, however, philosophy was the science of general principles which are behind all things. This was the case until the empiricists narrowed its sphere of activity and rendered it as one particular science among the others. They confined its subject to the thoughts, or the psychological life, of the individual. When Kant arrived on the scene, however, he expended great efforts to reconcile the notions of universality and specialisation.

Kant's attitude toward the doctrines of empiricism and rationalism was one of caution: he did not accept the broad claims of either of them, nor did he agree with the notion that the empiricist school of thought had been successful in defining the sphere of human knowledge. The truth is, our knowledge begins with experience but this does not mean that all knowledge is derived from it. Furthermore, it could be that empirical knowledge itself is not derived purely from experience, but, rather, represents something to which the mind incorporates the impressions of the senses and those things which are reflected in them. That is to say, perhaps empirical knowledge is the result of both the activity of the mind as well its integration of the sensory representations which are conveyed to us.

The claim made by the empirical school can be opposed on two grounds: firstly, the existence of general theories conceived in the mind

---

1 Article from *al-Majalla al-Jadida* February 1935

– such as a priori mathematical concepts – have no connection with experience, nor is it possible to explain them in the light of; secondly, these general theories possess the force of inevitability – their outcomes are predictable. Experience does not have this quality: experiential knowledge cannot itself attain the degree of certitude without rationality and the theories which provide what this requires. Let's consider the law of gravity. Now, to assert that all objects fall towards the earth is not warranted on the basis of experience because, however extensive one's experience may be, no one can have experience of all objects, even if every conceivable effort is made by an individual to test this claim against tens, or even hundreds, of objects. If we assert that it is a universal law then we are doing based upon a capacity other than experience. Thus, our knowledge comprises elements which have no connection to experience.

Furthermore, Kant did not accept the rationalist school of thought with regard to its claims that knowledge is the exclusive domain of the mind, and that rational principles are the source of all true human knowledge. Descartes, on the other hand, had advocated these notions and repudiated any kind of knowledge which was not, ultimately, derived from simple, intuitive ideas. He made the discovery of these ideas a priority of philosophy, and from them he would then draw conclusions about human knowledge, all of it, using the mathematical method.

Kant opposed this manner of thinking. He made a distinction between mathematics and philosophy, a distinction which was to pave the way for what was to come: the idea that human knowledge is not limited to the principles of rationality, but that much of it is gained through experience. Furthermore, he saw mathematics, as a whole, as having its origins in simple, rational principles from which the mind constructs what it wills and which hold true provided that they are viewed with the eye of reason.

This does not preclude concordance between rational principles and that which is experienced – no one is claiming that rationality is in opposition to the real. As for philosophy, its principles are concepts such as 'cause', 'effect', and 'essence'. To conceive of these requires inspection and factual evidence. Therefore, knowledge is not the exclusive property of either experience or rationality: it is a combination of the two. To Kant, the object of philosophy was to define a priori, rational ideas which govern knowledge and action, to elucidate how they are linked, and create a complete philosophical system out of them.

With regard to the theoretical and practical aspects of philosophy, the theoretical aspect defines the subject, that is to say, it specifies its character and its principles, while the practical, on the other hand, carries the matter into effect. Generally, philosophy is – in terms of theory and practice – both abstract and empirical. It is abstract insofar as it is predicated upon principles which are outside of experience, and empirical insofar as it abstracts its principles from experience.

Furthermore, with regard to abstract theoretical philosophy, this is philosophy in the true sense of the word. It is divided into two subcategories insofar as it pertains to the study of the general principles of thought – i.e., that which is known through logic – and also insofar as it pertains to the study of the relationship between ideas and things, which is metaphysics. It is a science of general and absolute intellectual principles with regard to its relationship to things and, for Kant, it would perform two functions. One of these is critique, which is preliminary and which predominates in his philosophy. The other is the linking of general principles as a means of facilitating the creation of a philosophical system. With regard to practical, or ethical, philosophy, on the other hand, this is both abstract and empirical. It is abstract because its goal is knowledge of rational principles with regard to freedom, i.e., the principle of duty, and it is empirical insofar as it investigates principles of wisdom and rights.

However, for Kant, the most important function of philosophy was critique; through critique he was able to closely examine the philosophical doctrines that had come before. He sifted out exaggerated and radical claims, ultimately producing a strong philosophy. Indeed, his contribution to the general field of philosophy is considered to be one of the most solid.

After Kant, philosophers inclined towards the gradual restoration to philosophy of its comprehensiveness, while retaining for it its distinctive character as a science. Johann Gottlieb Fichte was the first to give thought to the creation of a science for the sciences. His understanding of science was brilliant; he saw each science as having a substance and a form – the substance being the subject of the science, and the form being its logical method, like analogy in the mathematical sciences and induction in the natural sciences. His view of science involved the induction of facts, the deduction of principles, and the construction of theories; however, he was unconcerned about sharply defining either its subject or its method. He did not question, for example, as to why its subject has existence, he didn't inquire about the links connecting this subject to the subject matter of other sciences, and he didn't reflect about why one type of thinking was suited to it and not another. This is because the science which examines the subject matter of the sciences, and their methods, is philosophy. Thus, it comprises all of the sciences and specialises in the investigation of a subject which is particular to it.

But if philosophy has its own subject and method, then it in turn requires a science to study these, just as it studies the subjects and methods of the other sciences. However, to prevent this sequence going on and on ad infinitum, Fichte believed that the study of the subject of philosophy and its methods should be entrusted to philosophy itself. In this way philosophy would be the supreme science, or the science of principles – an idea which he attributed to Aristotle's definition of philosophy.

Friedrich Wilhelm Joseph von Schelling and Georg Wilhelm Friedrich Hegel maintained Kant's notion of philosophy as the science of absolute rational principles, and that of Fichte that philosophy is the science of the sciences. However, they also expanded the definition of philosophy's subject matter, elucidating it and bringing it into line with their view concerning the oneness of existence. They believed that subject and object, reality and idea, and nature and psyche, are as one in the absolute, or conceptual, sense. This is not the place to provide a detailed explanation concerning the abstruse elements of this philosophy, however; instead, it suffices to say that its meaning is that contrasting aspects of existence are one in essence, conceptually.

There are two ways of verifying this singularity: either we begin with the object, reality, and nature, in order to demonstrate that they – and the subject, the idea, and the psyche, which stand opposite to them – are conceptually one, or the opposite. Philosophy means, by these two approaches, that knowledge possesses oneness of being since its subject matter must comprise all existence, in which case it will be completely restored to its former state, as it was in the time of Plato. However, this will not prevent the existence of some contemporary views that revert to Locke's conception of philosophy as a science of the mind, like the view of Thomas Reid and that of Dugald Stewart.

Victor Cousin's view of philosophy did not go beyond that of Fichte or Hegel. His opinion came to fruition over the course of two stages of development. Firstly, in the year 1818 he stated that every truth contains that which raises it to the rank of truth, that every science possesses individual properties which set it apart from the other sciences, and that the distinctive merits of science are among the highest qualities that can be attained. So what then is truth? What is science? This is the subject matter of the science of the sciences, or philosophy, in other words. Cousin later he came to view the subject matter of philosophy as being more extensive and more comprehensive than he had previously. In 1828 he stated that philosophy was a science of thought, or thinking which thinks about itself and those elements of truth which it comprises, and that in this way it is aimed at logic and ideas which are useful, upright, and beautiful, insofar as everything goes back to thinking.

With regard to Théodore Simon Jouffroy, he regarded philosophical matters as being confined to questions, some of which are concerned with things, while the others are concerned with general principles. However, he considered these principles only in terms of their relationships with things inasmuch as they provide solutions, for he believed that every philosophical matter finds its solution in a rational or intellectual principle and that, in the end, it all goes back to the science of the mind.

As for the positivists, they believed that the time of philosophy had passed, seeing it as being a non-essential form of human thinking.

Philosophy entered a difficult period during these times; it came to be seen as superfluous tradition. They said that philosophy, in its true meaning, no longer had any place in the field of human knowledge. Philosophy had been in existence – and had been needed – since the days when contemplating elements of practical, human experience had been confined of those with the means to devote themselves wholly to it. Now, however, science was divided up into *sciences*, with each science representing a separate branch. Furthermore, each of these branches was constructed on a basis that excluded metaphysical issues from entering into its field of study.

Even at the summit of its glory, metaphysics didn't arrive at truths into which doubt never entered. Metaphysics continually sets out to resolve its methods without ever reaching a solution. In contrast to this, there is the positivist science; this is one of the branches of knowledge that reaches certainty in truth. It is reliable and convincing because it establishes certainties through scientific tests. This vindicates the view which asserts that the human mind does not exist to solve the metaphysical problems that elude it, but that it has the capacity to investigate practical matters and attain, through its investigation, the most reliable of conclusions.

Thus, science does not seek the absolute: it is relativistic. Scientists did not establish the relativity of science through rational criticism; they did so as a conclusion of the history of human knowledge. They stated that human reason, before it reached the positivist state, had passed through two prior states: the theological and the metaphysical. In the theological milieu reason was applied as a means of uncovering the essence of things and primary causes, and phenomena were interpreted according to the notion of a power higher than nature. During the metaphysical state, however, we find a clear change in how reason was conceived of: the distinctive, individual power is replaced by abstract forces which are present in the different phenomena and occasion them. As for the positivist state, reason's primary concern is to study phenomena, their interrelatedness, and discover their laws.

Through a summarisation of the views within philosophy we can understand that its meaning wavers between being the science of the sciences; the science of absolute, rational principles of thought and existence; and the science of the human mind. Thus, it is distinct from general science, on the one hand, as the science of the psyche by virtue of its study of psychological matters, and on the other hand by its ideas of universality and of the oneness of things, from which metaphysics emerged. Philosophy straddled these two approaches throughout the ages until Kant attempted to reconcile them. Through his focus on the psyche, he hit upon the absolute, rational principles. As for a response to the objective school of thought, it suffices to say that the subject matter of philosophy is not the same as that of science – this justifies the reasons for its existence. Furthermore, the success of science and its methods does not demonstrate that philosophy and its subject matter are invalid, or that its methods are faulty. Indeed, despite the success of science, and its ability to attain the most perfect results, nevertheless, it cannot cure the human soul of its yearning for knowledge. The truth of the matter is that there is a guiding light in science, and science has advantages, yet it does not convince the mind, which continues to strive after other questions which perplex it and which spur its investigation. These questions are those which spring from the innermost heart of the soul and which ensure – and will continue to ensure – the continued existence of metaphysics.

Science itself is truly a phenomenon to be investigated and contemplated. How, for example, did it come into existence? What are its causes and its objectives? And how does one determine its various methods? All of these questions necessitate a science which examines science itself from its different aspects. It is not enough that we find out about phenomena and attach these to various principles. There are other questions that are no less important or legitimate in terms of knowledge. What, for example, is the value of knowledge? We can know nothing, nor can we draw conclusions about a given matter, except through thinking. Will our knowledge accord with reality and the truth, or will it instead represent the delusions constructed and shaped by our thinking? Indeed, where is the evidence that distinguishes between actual truth and subjective fantasy that exists outside the realm of thought? All of these questions require a science which can investigate them and establish the truth of the matter.

These questions are philosophy's raison d'être. It will endure, therefore, as long as these questions remain, and as long as the soul, which prompts them, endures.

Psychology: Its Trends and Methods, Ancient and Modern[1]

Psychology, as an independent science, is a modern field of study. The psyche, however, is among the subjects which have attracted the attention of man since ancient times. Indeed, in ancient times this subject was considered as part of natural philosophy.

From Thales to Socrates

Prior to the era of Socrates, the prevailing tendency leaned entirely towards the natural sciences and the psyche, or soul, was conspicuously neglected. Nevertheless, the distinction between it and the body is very much an ancient one – one which death had lead man to make. Naturally, this conceptualisation of the soul was primitive, for it was believed to be a breath which seeps out through the mouth or through wounds. The ideas of the ancient philosophers did not significantly progress beyond such formulations. Neither Pythagoras' mathematics, nor the Eleatics' concept of oneness, represented abstract, spiritual essences; rather, the belief was that bodies were composed of an essence which was material in nature.

The fact is that in order for the creation of the science of the psyche to come about, man's attention first had to be directed towards it, rather than being entirely preoccupied with natural science. We can observe a general tendency toward subjective thinking in Greek intellectual life

---

1 Article from *al-Majalla al-Jadida* March 1935

which gradually advanced, little by little, from the time of Thales until the era of the Sophists.

In the arts, poetry developed; from the epic style came lyrical poetry and the theatrical poetry of drama. Ancient Greek drama began with the heroic tragedy, then came the religious tragedy and, lastly, the psychological tragedy. In terms of politics, democracy was founded upon aristocratic freedom of thought and the observance of traditions. As for philosophy, Pythagoras, Heraclitus, the Eleatics, and the Atomists, were in agreement that the senses are insufficient when it comes to uncovering the various aspects of true knowledge, but that this requires intellectual critique. Anaxagoras even distinguished between matter and the mind, conceiving of the intellect as a force of nature. When the Sophists arrived they came to see a connection between the creative mind and the mind of man.

All of these approaches were valuable. However, it was Socrates who was the first to turn the examination of the psyche into a philosophical method in its own right: it was he who focussed on it and gave it much of its importance. Nevertheless, we should not consider him as being among those who tried to dedicate a specific science to it. Socrates believed that knowledge of the psyche is the sum of all knowledge insofar as it guides us towards the principles of thinking and the fundamentals of ethics. To Socrates, knowledge of one's psyche is knowledge of logic and of truth at the same time.

Plato

The philosophy of Plato is expansive and comprises all things. The psyche was viewed as an organ of the body and it was studied as one of the subjects of natural science. According to Plato, within the world of perceptible things there is a centre which is the soul of this world; this is what creates order, life, and human knowledge, and from it springs forth all of the lower souls, such as those of human beings or of animals. The saying, 'Know thyself' did not come from Plato, but this does not detract from the brilliance of his investigations into the psyche. He made a distinction between the psyche and the body, and he perceived the psyche as having three parts which reside in the head, the heart, and the stomach, respectively. Furthermore, he spoke about the three degrees of knowledge and he elucidated the types of love, the theory of pleasure, the reasoning faculty and that of the senses. He explored all of these topics either through natural science or metaphysics.

Aristotle

Aristotle was the first person to direct particular attention towards phenomena of the psyche as observed within the scope of our consciousness. He saw in philosophy a sphere of scientific knowledge whose principles were in union but whose subjects varied. To him, the science of the psyche was one of the branches of natural science which was established upon the foundations of metaphysics – its method of analysis and of probation – but whose spirit derived from that which is beyond nature.

Contrary to Plato, Aristotle did not believe in the existence of a world soul as a living thing; however, he did acknowledge the existence of the lower souls of plants, animals, and human beings. To him the soul was the source of life, and in the human being were the following types: the nutritive soul, the sensitive soul, the volitional soul, and the rational soul. He viewed the rational soul as a soul which is more or less independent. In this respect he conducted stand-alone studies of the soul concerning perception, memory, sleep, and other things.

Epicureanism, Stoicism, and Neo-Platonism

The Epicurean school of philosophy fundamentally sought to pave the way for a science of ethics, which it saw as the best means for achieving its aim of living happily. For this reason, Epicureans viewed natural science as being subordinate to that of ethics, conceiving of the former as something which leads to the latter. Since psychology was a part of natural science, it was through this that its truths were derived. This is why we find that the theory of sensory perception is based on the atomist theory of nature, and that belief in freedom emanates from belief in causeless motion.

The Stoics possessed the same practical attitude which rendered all other branches philosophy subordinate to ethics, and for them psychology was a part of natural science. They held the view that the world is a living thing – an orderly body whose soul is God. However, their distinction between the spiritual and the physical was not established upon a firm philosophical basis. To the Stoics, man comprises both a soul and a body, and the soul's connection to the body is as that between the soul of God and existence. It is through this connection that man's will and power are manifested.

As for Neo-Platonists, their predominant theological idea was the belief that existence has a soul – a notion which had been held by both Plato and the Stoics before them. It is almost as if they viewed this soul as being the Holy Ghost of the Holy Trinity. According to Neo-Platonism, this soul comprised all of the lesser souls, even if they are unaware of the reason for their creation. Thus, the science of the human soul is wrapped up in the science of the earthly soul and its origins are in the science of the being.

From all of this we can understand that psychology, as a special science for the human mind, did not exist in ancient times. Aristotle, however, did came close to it through devoting himself to the study of the phenomena of the soul as a subject in and of itself, while other philosophers studied it through natural science, theology, or metaphysics. Saint Augustine of Hippo, however, took a considerable step with regard to this topic; it was he who said that the subject of philosophy is knowledge of God and the soul, and that in order to know the soul we must commune with it and not stray far from it. Furthermore, in his later writings he inclined towards subordinating psychology to divinity, thereby raising questions that were difficult to solve.

After this the Middle Ages arrived; this was an era in which the mind put its faith in tradition and shunned originality. Indeed, anything which is found to be exceptional during this period is due to the inspiration of Christianity on the minds of some philosophers. On the whole, however, we can say that the philosophers of these times directed most of their concern to interpreting the psychology of Plato, Aristotle and Saint Augustine, through a theological lens. Among the philosophers of this period were those who revived the theory of the 'world soul' that Plato and the Stoics had spoken of long before, and there were those who urged for endeavour and contemplation as a means of attaining a station in which the truth of the heart would be revealed. There were many, such as these sorts of thinkers, from whom nothing that we have discussed so far originated, nor did they add any significant contributions to the field of thought.

The Cartesian School

The intellectual rigidity of this era came to an end with the arrival of Descartes. It was he who gave new life to the world of thought, the effects of which did not fail to influence those philosophers who came after him. Descartes began his philosophy by questioning everything, even his own soul. But he ultimately cast this beyond doubt and made it a cause for certitude. So, is he considered to be a founding father of the science of psychology, as a science which investigates psychological phenomena? Descartes studied ideas. Among these he distinguished between those that are attributable to the senses, those that are produced in the imagination, and those that are intuited through our psyches. He spoke about the role played by the will with regard to both the arrival at truth and entanglement in error. He also spoke a great deal about the errors of the senses, but in all of this his approach was metaphysical.

This does not change the fact, however, that Descartes' scepticism paved the way for both modern philosophy and modern psychology. It was he who said that the psyche is the foremost truth and that this was his fundamental concern. He paved the way for the empirical psychology of Locke, who strove to discover the limits of human knowledge through his study of the mind. Furthermore, in his writings concerning desires and feelings he paved the way for the science of physiology which interprets psychological phenomena in light of the mechanics of the human body.

Nicolas Malebranche, however, was more akin to the psychologists than his teacher; it was he who said, in contrast to Descartes, that the psyche is more difficult to comprehend than the body, because it is not subject to the methods of mathematics. Despite this, however, he argued that the use of experimentation is indispensible in the understanding of the science of the psyche – in this way he distanced it from the field of metaphysics. Malebranche's studies on the imagination, memory, and random causes, paved the way for the associationist school of thought.

Baruch Spinoza agreed with Malebranche with regard to his view on the abstruseness of the psyche. He stated that knowledge of it does not come about through inner contemplation, but through deducing the nature of God. Furthermore, according to Spinoza, man is not an independent entity in the world of being; rather, he exists as a part within it – whatever laws apply to the whole also apply to him, and just as we know God, so to can we know the psyche. His book *Ethics* contains brilliant examinations of the rational faculties and sensory phenomena.

Gottfried Wilhelm Leibniz

This philosopher had a general philosophical system which was derived from his conception of the psyche. It is as though he adopted psychology as the basis of the formation of metaphysics. To Leibniz, existence was composed of psychic substances which burst forth with a spontaneous force. His approach was metaphysical and he studied an aspect of something only in terms of its relationship to the whole. Following on from Locke, he wrote a treatise on human reason in which, step by step, he interpreted his observations through metaphysics.

John Locke

Locke is the founding father of empirical psychology as a science of inner phenomena. It was he who applied inductive logic to the study of the human mind. He was the originator of an intellectual method in psychology which will endure as part of the field for all time. He

separated psychology from natural science and metaphysics. Furthermore, in his study of the mind he did not take up questions regarding
the essence of the psyche or its nature; instead, he contented himself
with investigating changes which occur in the psyche, or in the body,
and from which feelings and thoughts emerge.

David Hume

Hume followed Locke in adopting a method of internal observation,
and he assessed the difficulties he encountered in this. In the course
of such observation it is quite difficult to determine the sites of connectedness and of separation with regard to different phenomena.
Furthermore, it is a burdensome task to sustain one's concentration in
order to scrutinise an individual phenomenon – a sublime inspiration is
needed to shed light on the complexity of the psychological life. Hume
did not stop at such, however; he attempted to discover the principles
which preside over the psyche and govern its phenomena. There was
no cause for despair in this, however; astronomy which had previously
been a descriptive science had become a perfect science which could
reveal celestial laws. Hume believed that he had succeeded in finding
the general principle for the law of association, which he had formu-
lated according to the model of the law of gravitation existing in the
world of nature. It is for this reason that he is the founder of associationist psychology. Similarly, Thomas Reid also exemplifies this stance.
He was part of the Scottish Enlightenment which liberated psychology
from metaphysics, and logic also; this is what distinguishes him from
Locke and Hume, because the latter two maintained the view that psychology was a means for defining the human mind. Reid did, however,
understand the psyche as Locke had. To him it represented that faculty
we possess which remembers, which thinks, and which desires – its
properties can be known but not its essence, and the route to this
knowledge is by means of observation.

The French School

Among the philosophers of this movement were Pierre Paul Royer-Collard and Théodore Simon Jouffroy, who can both be considered as belonging to the Scottish school because they did not add anything new which was significant.[2] With regard to Victor Cousin, his horizons were expanded by his contact with the Germans who very clearly had a strong influence on him. He saw psychology as a means, believing that, through the study of phenomena, it would be possible to attain knowledge of their psychological origin, and from this origin he would be guided to knowledge of God. Thus, he made psychology a basis of metaphysics.

Maine de Biran opposed this approach. He said that, through the phenomena, he wanted to arrive at the principles. The aim of induction is, in fact, to elucidate the relationship between two phenomena, or the totality of phenomena, but it does uncover the essence. His basic idea comes from his separation between a being which is conscious of its self, in itself, and a thing which has no awareness of its self, but which can be subject to examination from outside. Therefore, according to de Biran, the method used in the natural sciences cannot be the same method for psychology. To him, the greatest error committed by those who see no need for this separation is that they confound psychic forces with physical causes. The physical causes are factors which the rational mind abstracts from phenomena, such as gravitation. When these thinkers did not make a separation between these and the psychic forces they concluded that the psychic forces were also abstractions which have no existential reality.

The truth is that we are ignorant with regard to the absolute psyche; however, between pure metaphysics and unadulterated empiricism we find a medium, which is contemplation, or the mental impulse, and which guides us through the psyche towards truths that are neither purely metaphysical nor uninformed by empirical observations. De Biran saw the will as being the foremost element, and the basis, of psychological life – he believed that it is the agent in knowing.

---

2 These French philosophers did not exactly belong to the Scottish Enlightenment, of course, but they were strongly influenced by philosophers associated with it.

Psychology in Germany

In England and France attempts were made to mix psychology with philosophy. In Germany, however, psychology remained subordinate to general philosophy. Kant's approach was not empirical like that of Locke, nor was it intuitive like that of de Biran; instead, he used critique. This was his method of choice in philosophical investigation, generally, and implicitly with regard to psychology. It was through critique that Kant discovered the general, absolute principles to which he subjected psychological phenomena, as well as the external phenomena which is the concern of other branches of science. In this respect, no method was particular to philosophy or to psychology, for psychology was merely a subsidiary aspect of philosophy.

In essence, this is similar to what we find among Fichte, Hegel and Schelling: that the psyche has its particular place in the sequence which connects the various things in existence to it. It is known by considering it as an organ within a common body. Thus, if it is known, it is possible for us to deduce, from our knowledge of it, the aspects of its progression and the manifestations of its activity.

Johann Friedrich Herbart likewise made it subordinate to metaphysics. He presented it as being the science of the psyche's mechanics whose method complied with that used in the mathematical sciences. To him the foremost question was: due to which mathematical laws do the phenomena of the psyche unite or repel one another?

Changes in the Subject of Philosophy and Its Approach

Subsequently, psychology moved towards a complete separation from metaphysics through the work of those who came after the associationists, thinkers such as John Stuart Mill, Alexander Bain, and Herbert Spencer, as well as the German naturalist psychologists, such as Gustave Fechner and Wilhelm Wundt. Psychology was no longer a science of the psyche; rather, it was the science of inner psychological phenomena and their connection to associated physical and physiological manifestations. It was not confined to being a positivistic science; however, it did attempt to discover psychological laws and was concerned with these principally in terms of their scientific import, as understood by the modern natural scientists. Before psychology had made principle synonymous with cause, now it assumed a new meaning and the horizons of its investigative field were expanded. It was no longer limited to the observation of the psyche; instead, it moved beyond this branching into study of various subjects which are among the most important sources for knowledge of the psyche, such as the study of animals, physiology, pathology, art, and history.

This does not mean, however, that psychology dispensed with the method of inner investigation. There was a need for objective research but this was not enough in itself – subjective analysis was also required. Consider how you enjoy various artistic masterpieces, for example. You can only achieve understanding of artistic creativity and experience its beauty through the aid of your feelings and your artistic openness. Inner contemplation is the foundation of psychological genius, but this is dependent upon the truth found in art, literature, and history, rather than conjecture and supposition.

And now, what are the modern orientations that have been prescribed by the various approaches, both subjective and objective? With regard to the subjective approach, this is a method of psychological inquiry whose value is recognised even by empiricists, even if some of the more radical among them – such as Vladamir Bekhterev and the adherents of the behaviourist school – have rejected it. It does for the gifted what analysis does for logicians and scientists in their research. Even if this approach pertains to the individual, and its verdicts don't attain the universality that characterises scientific conclusions, nevertheless, it gives empiricism its value – as Alfred Binet claimed – because, a physical effect does not inform us of the psychological condition causing it; an intermediary is required to explain it.

Introspection was developed in fundamentally new ways through the work of Henri Bergson and William James. They shifted away from the method of deconstruction and, instead, adopted a constructive approach: they moved away from studying the phenomena of the psyche bit by bit, and shifted their focus towards attempting to understand its essence all at once, as a self-existent unit. Bersgon claimed that as soon as we abandon the old modes, and free ourselves from the constrictions of language, the psyche will know through intuition. William James, on the other hand, stated that psychological states are not directly known, but rather, what is known is the total content of the individual's awareness, like that which is revealed to us in a given moment – and such a moment is, without a doubt, a happy one.

According to this understanding of the psyche knowledge of it is only attainable through a metaphysical approach. Consequently, psychology was confined to metaphysics, whether that was in terms of method, as has been examined, or subject matter. This is because the psyche began to stimulate interest beyond the investigation of phenomena, and the laws of their interdependence and their occurrence, which it had been limited to for some time. In this regard we have the words of Octave Hamelin who said that the psyche is an image of the truth of existence, as well as those of Jules Lachelier who said that psychology defines the essential, universal conditions of thought and existence. This is how psychology, with its complete reliance upon internal contemplation, came to be orientated in this way.

With regard to the objective approach, this is the approach which is presently adopted by the majority of those working in the field of psychology, such as Bekhterev, Ivan Pavlov, and the behaviourists, who completely disregard internal examination and instead rely solely upon scientific testing. Test an individual or an animal under varying conditions and observe the different responses. To the behaviourists, the psyche is nothing more than these responses. As for the notion of an independent consciousness which possesses certain characteristics, this is considered to be nothing more than an old and enduring error – something that was once referred to as 'the soul'. This objective approach which the institutes sometimes have recourse to is spreading in industrialised countries. From these have come laws of the utmost mathematical accuracy; yet, many in the field of philosophy, such as Bergson, are sceptical about their value in relation to psychology.

Whatever the case may be, this empirical approach is very useful because it trains the scientist to aim for complete accuracy, it accustoms him to persevere with determination, and it cautions him about making hasty generalisations – as Ribot has said. With regard to scientific testing in pathology, and human society in general, there is no doubt about how useful and productive it is, for people can become mentally ill and this is the subject matter of pathology. Pathology goes side by side with psychology; understanding illnesses and explaining their causes illuminates the dark recesses of the psyche and allows us to better understand human nature. This is the basis of the approach employed by Sigmund Freud.

Furthermore, psychological phenomena have social aspects which can influence us. But how does one uncover these social aspects, and to what extent do they affect one's psychological state? Émile Durkheim turned the matter on its head: it was he who said that the social phenomenon is the origin, and that one's frame of mind derives from, and is explained by, it. In this way, the true science of the human psyche is directed toward human society and objective, sociological phenomena are studied by means of scientific observation. Furthermore, it has also been said that a psychological phenomenon is nothing more than fantasy and delusion.

In light of all this, one can see that psychology branched out from philosophy and became an independent field. Subsequently, philosophy tried to bring it back into its fold. The new sciences, however, such as pathology and sociology, seized it – each seeking to annex it within their own field and assimilate it. Philosophy, however, only attempted this insofar as it found in psychology a fertile ground for its own investigations. As for the claims of the other sciences, they were inspired by a radicalism which is presently receding, withdrawing its claims and leaving behind what truth it had discovered. In all of this, knowledge continues along its course, profiting from the various experiments without aligning itself to them, nor permitting them to eliminate it.

Animal Life and Psychology[1]

Animals have a close connection to man which is both historical and beneficial. It is for this reason that they, among all created things, became the subject of human thinking. Initially, this thinking was primitive, but later it developed into philosophical investigation, and one of its foremost aims came to be to define the meanings of instinct and intelligence.

The legends of our ancestors indicate that they imagined that every created thing possessed a soul like that of man; that is to say, they made no differentiation between the human, the animal, and the plant – nor, indeed, in relation to that which is inanimate. Furthermore, among their beliefs was the notion that souls transmigrate from one body to another. This ancient belief found its way into philosophy. It is encountered in the philosophy of the Pythagoreans which states that souls differ in their fates after death according to what they deserve: some souls live a life free from material existence, and some reside in new human bodies, or those of animals, as a form of punishment imposed upon them which they must endure. This theory indicates that souls are equal in their nature, but that they differ in terms of station, as denoted by the bodies in which they reside, which may be those of humans or of animals. This was also the view held by Empedocles, but he believed that souls might also transmigrate into plants, because the soul of a plant possessed the same nature as the soul of an animal or a human. Anaxagoras, on the other hand, was the first person to make

---

1 Article from *al-Majalla al-Jadida* April 1935

a distinction between souls. He said that although the mind differs in terms of its volume among the various created things – i.e., the human, the animal, and the plant – nevertheless, it does not differ in terms of its nature.

In short, before the arrival of Socrates, philosophy tended to consider the souls of humans and animals – and sometimes those of plants – as being of one nature. If any philosopher of this period distinguished between these souls his distinction between them was incidental, being in reference to station or speech, not to nature or essence. When Socrates arrived, however, he differentiated between instinct and the rational mind. He said that divine providence arranges the natural instincts for us, which are non-thinking. Parents, for example, seek to perpetuate themselves through their children, and creatures seek to avoid death and to stay alive. This providence protects both the human and animal alike; however, there is greater abundance and perfection in the lot of human beings. God blessed us with a mind which is more consummate in its intelligence because it is man, and man only, that worships God, prophesies the divine secret, and strives for knowledge – among all living creatures it was man who was likened to the gods.

With regard to Plato, he divided the human soul into the rational soul, the spirited soul, and the appetitive soul. He believed that the soul of the animal is a fallen human soul. Following this logic, the soul of the plant should then be considered as a fallen animal soul; however, Plato did not accept this conclusion, because he didn't believe that it was possible for the human soul to reside within a plant. The root of his thinking was that souls descend from the heavens into bodies and that the virtuous among them are purified in this life before ascending back from where they came. As for those souls which have gone astray – within whom the light of rationality has gone out – they inhabit various bodies in accordance with their offenses. Such a soul may occupy the body of a woman, or it may occupy that of an animal, for the animal soul is a human soul whose sins have caused it to be transformed.

To Aristotle, the soul was the source of life. He viewed the soul of the animal as the sensitive soul and he analysed this soul in order to know what differentiated it from human souls and those of plants.

He said that the animal possesses sensory perception; this necessarily means that it experiences pleasure and pain, which are associated with desire. To Aristotle, desire is what induces movement and it is awakened by direct sensation, just as it is by sensory imagination. The latter is a mental image which is linked to sensation, and which it sometimes invokes in the absence of external stimuli. It is different from the human memory which is distinguished by the will and the effort it expends in memorising things – this is also present in animals, but they are completely bereft of rationality and free will. However, Aristotle did differentiate between instinct and animal intelligence. In the case of instinct, sensation, desire, and movement combine and blend together – on this point they do not differ from plants. As for the higher animals, however, they resemble man insofar as choice plays a role in their lives, as does sensory imagination and memory.

The Stoics rejected the notion of animals having any kind of rational intelligence. They conceived of instinct as an agent of nature which is possessed by plants and animals for achieving its vital goals. They believed that plants and animals are governed by nature which ordains a single purpose: to stay alive and produce offspring. It is true that plant life may differ from animal life, but such differences do not alter the essence of the argument in any way. Neither sensation nor desire enter into the life of plants. Nature endows animals with sensation and desire in order to further their growth in ways different to plants; nevertheless, the gifts possessed by animals are still subject to, and still serve, the aims of nature. The behaviours of all animals are blind, thoughtless, and uncalculated: they know neither resolve nor hesitation.

Plutarch responded to the Stoic's view by saying that the claim that animals have no rational intelligence is meaningless, because rational intelligence, like many other things, has different degrees, and animals have their own portion of it. As for the argument which denies that animals possess rational intelligence because it does not reach the degree which it reaches in man, he compares this to denying that humans have the capacity to see and hear simply because there are some animals that can see and hear better than human beings. Animals can be trained, they respond positively to reward, and they have sensory perception; this would mean that they must have sensory imagination and memory, of some sort. Furthermore, affected by the impulses of love and hatred they are able to anticipate what lies ahead and, thereby, satiate these urges. This view is considered to be a return to older views, and it too was succeeded by another return to the past that we find within Neo-Platonism, which takes up the theory of the transmigration of souls and that of the universal soul of existence. According to this, all souls are of one nature but are separated from the aforementioned universal soul. They descend and enter various bodies, be it that of an animal or human, a sage or a fool. Then, after their span of earthly life has expired they return to the cosmic, universal soul. The souls of animals are souls which have lost the light of rationality that radiates within but which continues to have sensory perception and carnal appetites.

Following the spread of Christianity, a number of evangelists – such as Tatian, Arnobius, and Lactantius – came to be well-known for the new idea that it was only Christians who were distinguished from animals, while non-Christians were no more than animals that incidentally possessed the ability to speak. With regard to Saint Augustine, he went back to Aristotle's view that man has life just as plants do, and sensory perception as animals do, but that man alone has been blessed with rationality. The animal has a soul insofar as it behaves in ways that bring about what is good and beneficial for it. The animal has memory and imagination, and it can dream, but rationality plays no part in its life.

Aristotle's view remained influential among Christian thinkers throughout the Middle Ages. The view of Saint Thomas Aquinas concerning the animal soul is also worth mentioning here: he believed that it comprises the imagination, the senses, the estimative faculty, and the memory. So what is meant by 'the estimative faculty'? On this point he said that the bird does not gather straw out of a love for its beauty; rather, it does so in order to build its nest. Thus, the objective here is not brought about by the sensory perception: the bird brings it about by means of its estimative faculty. It does not estimate by means of a rational mind; rather, instinct does for it what reason does for man.

Subsequently, the European Renaissance arrived and a fierce revolt flared up against the doctrines of medieval scholasticism. Two intellectual stances gained ascendency: a love of the natural world and a zeal for life. It was Giordano Bruno who said that everything was living and that all created things, from the celestial bodies in the heavens to the stones of the earth, sense to some extent, even if this is hidden from us. Furthermore, to Bruno, the animal was only different from man in terms of degree, and its instinct, which protects it, is another form of human intelligence. On this point, Michel de Montaigne even went as far as praising animal instinct and its impact on the human mind. Like the wondrous aspects of the human mind, animals have marvellous and astonishing attributes – attributes of dazzling design reveal the exaltedness of the maker, and if the creation is sublime, then its maker must be greater and more sublime. Furthermore, in much of their activities and techniques, animals are superior to us in terms of proficiency and skill. Why is it said that they are driven to act by an irresistible force of nature? Instinct is no more than a word in people's minds; the truth is that animals think, make comparisons, and draw conclusions – and they outperform us in all of these. If some insist on attributing the actions of animals to irresistible nature, then, by doing so, they increase the exaltation of the animal insofar as they hold the view that nature has a loving inclination toward animals, that it surrounds them with its care, and allows them to accomplish, with little difficulty, things that we as humans are incapable of doing through extensive reflection and deep contemplation; this thwarts the instinct by merging it with rationality.

Descartes also gave his opinion on this topic: he viewed the movements of animals as being automatic. The animal cannot have a rational mind because it is unable to speak: were it to possess even the smallest of rational minds it would be capable of speaking. Furthermore, its actions do not indicate the presence of rational intelligence, because even if an animal demonstrates remarkable proficiency in terms of its own particular skills, nevertheless, it is helpless when it comes to all of the other skills.

What then are animals? To Descartes animals are machines of

perfect design, and it is the work of the moving parts of those machines that astonishes us. However, he regarded sensory perception as being beyond the capability of animals, since in his philosophy he had made a complete separation between thought and substance. To him, sensory perception was an accessory to thinking; thus, if animals were to have sensory perception, then they would also be able to think and, therefore, have immortality. This view spread among thinkers of the 16th century, such as Blaise Pascal, Pierre Nicole, and Antoine Arnauld.[2] To these thinkers animals do not experience fear, pain, or desire; rather, the driving force behind all of their actions is nature.

Bussy attempted to reconcile the mechanists and the advocates of sensualism.[3] He stated that the animal is a machine, because if external factors are brought to bear on it, it lacks the will to resist their influence. Nature produced a set of factors that influence through pleasure, and another set which do so through pain. From this he drew the conclusion that sensory perception is closely associated with the activities of an animal without being a cause for them.

With regard to Leibniz, he rejected the division between man and animal. His metaphysical theory conceived of being as having a simple essence. At its lower part this essence is composed of inanimate matter, while at its higher part it is composed of rationality – it is a continuous chain without a gap. To Leibniz, plants and inanimate things are reactive, animals use their senses, and humans are endowed with the reasoning faculty. He saw the difference between reactivity, sensing, and reasoning, as being a difference in degree, composition, and capability, rather than there being an absolute division, like the complete separation between thought and substance as conceived by Descartes. Thus, to Leibniz, the animal possesses a sensory soul which consists of the sensations that it receives, in

---

2 These three philosophers were all born, and lived, in the 17th century, not the 16th.

3 It is unclear to whom b-w/ū-s-y/ī (بوسى) refers. Not untypically, Mahfouz provides no forename. I have taken the liberty of using 'Bussy' in the text. Mahfouz, Naguib, Ḥawla l-Adab wa-l-Falsafa, Cairo, 2003, p. 107

addition to a memory, to which it is connected and which preserves it. Furthermore, it is endowed with a kind of rational faculty; however, this rational faculty is experiential rather than being driven by general, necessary principles.

With regard to de Condillac, his theory was novel and more influential. He believed that animals are not inherently endowed with anything as a result of nature, but that they acquire these things. Therefore, that which we call 'instinct' is actually the outcome of experience; it is essentially habit which is developed by mental capabilities. We should not imagine that the higher animals are driven to develop their different skills through a guiding, natural instinct. No, little by little, they gain mastery in these through experience and practice, just as humans learn to suckle, to recognise things, and to judge distances. But what of the claim that an animal's habits are repetitious and uniform? De Condillac's answer to this is that every species of animal pursues particular objectives and the body of each animal is endowed with particular means for achieving these. It is for this reason that it behaves in ways which are similar.

The observer will deny this view, however, for instinct cannot be taught. Scientists such as Jean-Baptiste Lamarck, Spencer, and Darwin modified this view. To them, instinct is not so much an individual habit as it is a habit which a species acquires gradually over the passage of time. The hypothesis which all three of these scientists employed was that of evolution: that there is interrelation between the organic anatomy and instinct. They did not stop at this however, but pursued their respective inquiries further. Lamarck stated that instinct is essentially an inherited habit, one that evolves due to the organism's interaction with its environment. One of the results of this interaction is that certain parts of the organism grow larger through use, while others atrophy due to neglect. According to Lamarck, animals inherit their ultimate form following these processes of growth or atrophy, with regard to their characteristics. Furthermore, whenever the conditions changed, so too did the habits and the characteristics of the organisms; thus, new habits were passed on, emerging as inherited instincts.

Spencer took this hypothesis and interpreted instinct and inherited habits as Lamarck had done. He found no essential difference between instinct and intelligence. In the case of instinct, life is uncomplicated, and stimuli are limited; thus, responses are simple and limited, becoming automatic through repetition. In the case of intelligence, however, the organism's life is complicated: influencing factors are manifold and, consequently, responses also vary, inasmuch as the continuous repetition which would produce automatic responses is impracticable. Thus, the organism possesses a general tendency to respond according to differing circumstances – this is intelligence.

Darwin, however, was not convinced that instinct should be interpreted in terms of heritability and habit. Among the various instincts, such as those of bees, for example, there is also that which causes every finely-worked wonder of which habit, despite its capability, is unable to make or fashion. Darwin believed that instinct could be correctly explained through understanding the origination of species, which occurs through individual difference, the struggle for existence, and natural selection. All things struggle with one another on account of life, and success is only attained through survival. Instinct is essentially nothing more than a distinctive trait brought about in the organism by chance. The advantage it confers is determined according to the circumstances: if the trait is desirable then it will spread through hereditary transmission. Accordingly, the origin of every evident system and organisation in life is down to the susceptibility of the organism, and the conditions of the environment, to chance.

These explanations are scientific. Science attempts to discover a mechanical explanation for nature. For this reason, science welcomes the theory of evolution, because it does not assume any hypothesis is final. The philosophers, however, were not convinced by this; they introduced final causes. The philosophies of Hegel, Schopenhauer, and Karl Robert Eduard von Hartmann are not like the empirical philosophies which explain instinct as the mechanism of blind nature, nor are they like the spiritual philosophies which try to explain it in light of higher faculties. They view instinct as acting according to a purpose of which it is unaware; in this sense it resembles the impulse of nature itself.

According to all of this, the contrast between intelligence and instinct is absolute, though they may come together, as in the case of man. However, the empiricists see a reflexive, mechanical impulse in instinct, and they consider the rational mind itself to be a form of it. With regard to the metaphysicians, to them instinct is an idea which evolved a mechanical form, and which became hidden within its subject. The direction of investigation took a turn in the modern era; the methods of animal psychology were revised and it branched out as a subject. Presently, knowledge of instinct's origin is not important, nor is the approach of studying animals as something analogous to man. The reliable method is to observe the animal and objectively interpret each phenomenon within the context of instincts while being cautious about attributing a given phenomenon to some higher faculty and, in this way, to gradually advance the study of the lower types of creatures. Jacques Loeb held that an animal's behaviour differed in its types because of difference in its causes; he referred to these as 'tropisms', which are very simple movements that arise from natural, or chemical, factors. This means that they are not physiological, and are occasioned by the influence of alkalis in the makeup of the organism's body.

However, not all animal behaviour there can be attributed to these movements. Loeb goes on to say that the organism is endowed with what he calls the 'the discrimination of sensory perception'. An organism may be drawn to natural energy, such as a source of light, for example, then, if the light level is altered, it will change its direction, oscillating like a pendulum before reverting to its original course. This change is caused by the change in sensation, or the differentiation between the former sensation and the subsequent one.

Loeb also ascribed thoughts to animals. These are formed by an interconnected system of sensations possessed by the animal, which we can correctly term as 'memory'. This is one of the causes and driving forces behind animal movement. This view of Loeb had two criticisms levelled against it:

1. Bieth's critique rejected the notion that animals possessed any

psychological life.[4] He did not accept that either feelings or thoughts were present in them.

2. Herbert Spencer Jennings' critique did not accept the afore-mentioned notion of tropisms. In his mind the organism does not perform simple movements like these; rather, it moves by its own power, devoid of feelings of either pleasure or pain. He attributes tropisms to reflex movements, i.e., reflexes. These reflex movements consist of agitation which is accompanied by movements; but this a nervous agitation, and movement is no different from that which we term 'tropisms'.

Ivan Pavlov conducted many experiments on animals which increased the wealth of our knowledge about reflexes and led to a concept concerning the origin of instinct. Many scientists attribute the instincts to reflexive movements. They do not see behaviours in these which fully serve to preserve the animal; indeed, Marshall has shown that insects may kill themselves, for example.[5] However, this has not prevented some philosophers, such as Bergson, from putting forth final-istic explanations for instincts. Bergson rejected the view of those who assign an objective to life, who believe that this is known prior and that the means for its accomplishment are arranged. To him, the source of life, and of evolution, is a creative leap, and instinct is one of the means which facilitates this leap.[6] Furthermore, intelligence of one of the means created by the life force to achieve its objectives. Intelligence differs from instinct. Their respective modes are not the same, for while intelligence uses tools, instinct uses the organs and shapes them.

---

4 It is unclear to me to whom *b-y/ī-th* (بيـث) refers. Not untypically, Mahfouz provides no forename. I have taken the liberty of using 'Bieth' in the text though this may be incorrect. Mahfouz, Naguib, *Ḥawla l-Adab wa-l-Falsafa*, Cairo, 2003, p. 111

5 It is unclear to whom Mahfouz is referring here; he again provides no forename. It may be a reference to Marshall Hall (1790–1857), an English physiologist of some note. Mahfouz, Naguib, *Ḥawla l-Adab wa-l-Falsafa*, Cairo, 2003, p. 112

6 This expression 'creative leap' (*wathba khāliqa*) probably refers to Bergson's well-known concept of *élan vital*. Mahfouz, Naguib, *Ḥawla l-Adab wa-l-Falsafa*, Cairo, 2003, p. 112

The essence of this remark is that the progress of psychology is due, in large part, to its empirical methods that study behaviour objectively, and which involve conducting various experiments on animals. It asks: how do they know to choose the known path and avoid traps? How do they overcome various difficulties? How is it that can they can open sliding bolts, and so forth? In this way psychologists uncover the mentality of the animal, assess its intelligence and the circumstances surrounding its acquisition of habits. However, we mustn't ignore the difficulties involved in these approaches. Explanation is difficult and seldom clear to the extent that it is entirely convincing. Furthermore, it can be perplexing in the face of questions for which there is no answer. For example, what makes one animal adopt certain behaviours as distinct from others? Why does it tend to repeat those behaviours which are beneficial and which accomplish their aim, even though the animal is unaware of what the benefit is?

The truth is that these empirical methods have benefitted us enormously in helping us to uncover the particulars of animal life. Yet, this does not solve our philosophical questions concerning the origin of instinct and its nature, nor does it satisfy teleological hypotheses which endure as the ultimate solution to which thinkers return when bewilderment torments them, as Bergson did.

The Senses and Sensory Perception[1]

A study of sensory perception comprises two questions: firstly, what is our connection to the external world? This question is one of the concerns of the empirical psychology. And secondly, what is it that we know of the external world? This subject falls under the critique of knowledge.

The philosophers of the past studied the senses and attempted to critique knowledge. However, it would be impossible to comprehend these attempts were it not known that none of philosophers prior to Socrates – or more correctly, prior to the Sophists – doubted the role undertaken by the thinker when it comes to knowledge, nor asked himself this question: is that which we experience the true reality, or is it a world in whose construction, formation, and alteration, the senses participate according to their inclination?

With regard to explaining sensory perception, the prevailing opinion at that time was that it consisted of the conjunction of similar elements. The oldest explanation we have for sensory perception is that of Alcmaeon of Croton who said that the head is the seat of the soul and that sensations reach it by means of conduits which connect it with the sensory organs. In this way sensation occurs when the properties of things are conveyed to the head. The most important of his preoccupations was his attempt to describe the mediums which transmit sensations. The claim that sensation occurs due to similar elements was not universal, however, even if it was the prevailing view. Heraclitus

---

1 Article from *al-Majalla al-Jadida* May 1935

and Anaxagoras believed that it was produced by opposing elements rather than ones which were alike, for like does not affect like insofar as it produces no change. We can feel the air, for example, when its temperature is different from that of our bodies.

One of the ancient theories which is worthy of mention is that of Empedocles. He believed that bodies had minute holes and that they emit substances which are so small they cannot be seen. He believed that sensation comes about because these substances detach and join up with others which are like them in the holes of neighbouring bodies. Furthermore, the holes differ and only those substances which correspond to the given hole may gain entry to it.

The theory of atomism, which is attributed to Democritus and Leucippus, explains sensations as being physical changes which are occasioned by contact with, and touching, external objects. But how does sensation occur if there is distance separating the subject and the object? In this instance it is explained by the diffusion which flows out the affecting body and spreads to the affected body, reaching the intended organs and producing sensation.

The majority of these philosophers inclined towards critique in their differentiation between knowledge and sensory perception. However, none of them attributed truth to either thought or the thinker; rather, they asserted that it is relative. Here it should be mentioned that it is Democritus to whom the credit for distinguishing between the principal properties and secondary properties belongs. It was he who said that the properties of the body can be broken down according to quantity, size, and shape, and to the interrelation of atoms of which they are composed. However, these vary insofar as some of them – such as weight and density – are recognised directly from the nature of their atoms. As for the others – such as colour and temperature – these vary according to variation in how the atoms mix together. The Sophists were the first to assert that knowledge varies among individuals and that it is relative. Protagoras stated that everything is relative and denied absolute rationality. According to this view, all sensory knowledge results from the encounter between the thinker and the subject; neither sensation nor that which is sensed possess actual truth, and a given experience is nothing more than something which occurs due to contact between two phenomena. The individual is the centre of things; thus, knowledge is relative.

This philosophy had an effect on Plato when he encountered it. He said that Protagoras viewed things which are sensed as originating from contact between the subject and the object. He stated that, while they do not express the truth of things, they may express a token of it. So what is sensation?

According to Plato, the world influences those elements of the body which it resembles. Sensation occurs when an external stimulus reaches the soul. Furthermore, the difference between things which are sensed goes back to difference in the activity taking place within the body. He also discussed the physiology of the senses, saying that the sense of touch extends over the body occasioning common sensations such as hotness, coldness, heaviness, and lightness. He regarded taste and smell as being intermediaries between touch and the higher senses: those of hearing and sight. In his analysis of the organ of sight he found that the light of the eye has an effect on sensory perception, and from this he concluded that perception is influenced by a factor which is subjective. So what is the value of rational knowledge?

Time and space represent two existential realities, but the reality of things which are sensed is not stable; thus, it is impossible to determine. Sensory knowledge represents the first step on the road towards knowledge of the ideal; it is by virtue of rationality that transcendence over that which is perceptible through the senses takes place.

As for Aristotle, he conceived of sensory perception as something that exists potentially, but not in effect, unless the conditions for sensation are fulfilled.[2] The conditions for this are existence of the thing which is sensed and the provision of sensory organs. Sensory perception extends throughout the body which possesses designated organs,

---

2 Mahfouz provides a footnote in his text, translated here: 'According to Aristotle, that which exists potentially is that which does not exist in effect; however, it can exist if conditions are right.' Mahfouz, Naguib, Hawla l-Adab wa-l-Falsafa, Cairo, 2003, p. 118

including the heart, which is the centre where all impressions end up. Aristotle divided properties that are sensed into three categories:

1. Special properties which are sensed only by certain sensory organs and not others, such as colours, which are sensed by sight.
2. Properties that are jointly sensed by the organs, such as movement and calmness, though each organ involved may sense these in their own particular way.
3. Concomitant properties which are not sensed directly but in conjunction with other things at the same time. An example of this is when you see the colour of something and taste its flavour at the same time. Then, if you subsequently see its colour again, this will cause you to re-experience its flavour. This crossover among the sensations explains why the senses are deceptive.

Sensation is the psyche's propensity to receive sensory forms without their substance. But how does the perceptible property fit into this scheme? It acts in collaboration with the organ and the thing which is sensed, or, in the words of Aristotle, its potentiality exists in both the organ and the thing – if it exists in effect, it exists in the organ. Sensory perception communicates the truth of things to us, but these vary in terms of substance, so rationality tries to work out their essential meaning. Thus, for Aristotle sensory perception represented something which gives an intimation of truth, rather than a mere illusion.

Epicurus was influenced by Democritus in his theory concerning the physiology of the senses. He critically examined them and advanced the following proofs by which he confirmed the veracity of the senses:

1. The senses are passive: they receive that which is external, no more, no less. If you perceive the colour red, then it must exist externally.
2. Sensation is a direct experience. It involves neither reflection nor thought, and it conveys its message reliably.

3. We have to trust the senses because we don't have the means
   to verify them. Thinking is unable to verify them as being true
   insofar as thinking itself cannot exist outside of them.

The Stoics similarly put their trust in the senses. To them, each truth
is physical inasmuch as it perceived by one of the senses. However,
they conceived of sensory perception as being an active force – that
is to say, they illustrated the role played by the will in knowledge. The
external thing affects the soul and leaves behind a form within it – this
is passive in nature – it is as though knowledge is not attainable unless
the faculty of constructive perception is connected with the external
object. Perception recognises certain characteristics as belonging to a
specific thing and in this way distinguishes between different things; it
is a force for clarification and dismisses doubt.

In the Middle Ages thinkers mistakenly attributed the theory of Epicurus to Aristotle; however, they asked the question: how do the forms
arising from matter affect the soul when the latter has no physicality?
Their answer to this was that these forms affect the sensory organs,
then, through the power of the soul they are transformed into spiritual
forms.

Descartes attributed sensory perception to the union of the soul and
the body. He recognised seven senses:

1. The internal sense which deals with sensations within the body,
   such as hunger, for example.
2. The five senses which are concerned with external things.
3. Desires.

The important aspect of Descartes' theory of sensory perception is
that it acknowledges the sensory nerves as being the principal agents
in sensation instead of the organs. It is not the eye which transmits light
and colour: it is the optic nerves that do this. These consist of conduits
which are filled with a substance like highly sensitive fire which speed-
ily conveys the external impression, carrying it to the pineal gland in
the head, which is the principal seat of the soul.

What is the value of sensory knowledge? Descartes strongly believed in rational knowledge. On this point he said that the clear, outstanding idea formulates its subject matter faithfully. If this were not so then God must have created our minds to believe that we can recognise the truth while seeing only a mirage, in which case God would be a deceiver – something which he is far above. To Descartes, the attributes of God guarantee rational knowledge. Sensory knowledge, however, is neither clear nor distinguished. It is not indicative of existing things; rather, it is indicative of the various forces which the perceptible world is composed of.

Descartes believed that objects influence the psyche and occasion sensation. When Malebranche came along he was perplexed by the explanation for an object's influence on the psyche. He asked himself how is it possible for an object to influence the psyche when they are both completely different in terms of their essence. Following from this he was driven to formulate his theory of random causes. According to his view the psyche does not affect the object in a direct way.[3] We do not see the sun, for example; rather, there is a thought of it in the psyche. So where does this thought come from?

According to Malebranche, God is the creator of everything; he created all things and all thoughts. Therefore, if he occasions an object to affect our brains, he creates a thought in our psyches which corresponds with it. Sensations are usually mysterious because their purpose is not knowledge but to ensure survival of the body. So, is there any evidence that an exterior world, which our senses encounter, actually exists? According to Malebranche there isn't, because God, who creates thoughts, and existing things, can do without creating them. However, divine revelation is proof that the material world exists, insofar as material things are spoken of in religion.

With his tendency toward empiricism, Locke freed psychology from metaphysics. According to him, sensory perception occurs when a

---

3 This sentence appears to be muddled according to the context. The terms 'psyche' and 'object' should probably be reversed, i.e., 'According to his view the object does not affect the psyche in a direct way.' Mahfouz, Naguib, Ḥawla l-Adab wa-l-Falsafa, Cairo, 2003, p. 122

sensation within a sensory organ reaches the psyche. Perception is a passive force that necessarily occurs when our senses encounter a given thing. Locke spoke about the perceptible properties and their categories. There are properties which are particular to an organ, such as colour, for example, and others which are jointly experienced by two senses or more, such as space and movement. He believed that the senses conveyed to us the impressions of things which have an external reality. From this he concluded that perception is involuntary and that some of the senses confirm the impressions of other ones. Furthermore, he said that the primary properties are inseparable from the things, such as solidity and dimension; secondary ones, on the other hand, such as colour and smell, don't possess actual truth.

Berkeley rejected this division because he believed that we encounter the primary and secondary properties through the same senses, for how can we rightly determine that the primary properties are true yet reject the secondary ones? He believed that all of the sensations are states within the soul, but not only this, that God directly creates them within us without the mediation of the external world. Did Malebranche not similarly say that being is unnecessary in the creation of thoughts? Let us eliminate this from our consideration and envision all being as composed of connected sensations fashioned by God – nothing except a collection of sensations which experience connects to habit. This is the philosophy known as 'idealism'.

Hume completed the philosophy of Berkeley; he went to the end of the road that Malebranche had begun to pave for idealism, as well as the empiricism begun by Locke. He was sceptical about the reality of primary properties; or rather, he made primary and secondary properties equal. Although Berkeley claimed that it is God who arranges sensations according to his laws, and that we only possess an internal thought, Hume had doubts about the reality of this argument. He interpreted the laws of sensation in the light of habit and experience, or by the laws of associationism.

The difficult task that Kant set for himself was finding a way to eliminate this doubt. For this to be possible, he believed it necessary to distinguish between two components of knowledge: matter and form. Matter is the element which is numerous and varied, while form represents the principles of thought by which things are comprehended. It was on the basis of this approach that he addressed the issue of sensory perception. He said that external perception is one of the forms of the mind. As for the external world, Kant identified this as space. It consists of the connection between inner sensations and one of the forms of the mind; it is only in this way that it can comprehend things. So, are we to understand from this that Kant rejected the existence of an external world which is real in itself and that he is an idealist?

The answer to this question is 'No'. Up until this point we have discussed his views concerning form in the context of perception, but there is also the issue of matter. This is the external subject whose essence we cannot comprehend; we can only know it through the forms of the mind. However, this does not preclude the existence of matter. To summarise his claim we can say that he believed that there are realities which are external, but that we cannot perceive these as they actually are in their essence.

As a result of this claim's extravagance, it was immediately disregarded by Reid, who was a strong advocate of common sense. He had first examined perception from the psychological angle, describing in detail the physiological processes which accompany perception, occurring within the sensory organ and the brain. He made a distinction between sensation – which is a subjective feeling – and perception, which is cognizance. As for the critical aspect, he rejected the claim that the things which are in our psyches are forms and thoughts because he had doubts about this. Instead, through his ideas about common sense, he advocated the notion of direct perception. But what is the meaning of perception?

Perception is the conception of something, accompanied by a firm conviction that this thing really exists. It is a direct conviction, and not the result of contemplation. So what is the relationship between sensation and perception? In what ways are they in opposition, and in what ways are they of one nature? Reid did not claim that he had the answer to this question, but he did not dismiss it either; it represented something to which all must be resigned, or to which common sense must resign itself.

There were two prevailing trends in the French school of thought: on one hand, there was the tendency toward logic and, on the other, there was a tendency toward exalting the importance of the will with regard to the process of perception. Antoine Destutt de Tracy said that activity is essential in order to perceive external existence. De Biran confirmed this view insofar as he believed that the sensory organ arose in relation to its being subject to the will for activity. Accordingly, there would be a gradual progression from organic sensations, culminating in the tactile sensation in the hand, because, like most of the senses, it is active. Furthermore, it was his opinion that the principal expression of consciousness is this will to activity. To de Biran this consisted of two things: the will, and the resistance of the moving organ. The resistance is recognised by mind, and knowledge of the mind requires knowledge of that which is not of the mind. In other words, knowing the logical definition of something requires also knowing the definition of its opposite, like being and non-being, and so forth.

This is undoubtedly a logical way of thinking; however, a clearer explanation can be found in the work of Victor Cousin. He claimed that the principle of causality leads us to knowledge of the external world. To Cousin, there had to be a cause for the sensory changes that take place within us; when we are not their cause – that is to say, when there is evidence that they take place without our will – then they must be caused by something external. In this way, sensory knowledge accords with rational knowledge.

The study of the senses made huge advances due to natural science and physiology. Natural science studies and determines the natural causes behind sensation – such as waves, the atmosphere, and ether – and explains their ordered interactions, which sensation translates into its mental language. Furthermore, it supports the hypothesis concerning the oneness of natural forces spoken of by Democritus. As for physiology, it studies the nervous system and determines the stimuli affecting the organs prior to sensation. Physiology distinguishes between the special nerves for sense and the nerves pertaining to movement. It gives explanation for the particular organs and detailed description concerning their systems. With regard to the brain, physiology is still trying to determine its complex centres for the various senses. Furthermore, physiology has set forth empirical evidence for the oneness of natural forces and the relativity of the senses. It has shown that a single cause produces various sensations when it affects the different senses. If, for example, you were to apply an electrical current to the auditory nerves, then you would hear a noise, and if you apply the same current to the optic nerves you would see a light. Whichever sensory organ you apply it to you will experience the particular sensation associated with that organ. On the other hand, different causes can produce a single sensation even in relation to a single sensory organ. There are small receptors in the skin, for example, which sense coldness, and others which sense heat. If you were to take a thin piece of wire and touch one of the points which sense cold with it you will feel coldness. Now, if you were to heat it in fire and then touch exactly the same spot, then, again, you would also feel coldness.[4]

These advances were brought about by applying the methods of natural science and physiology to sensation. Attempts were made to determine the link between physiological and natural phenomena on the one hand, and that between psychological phenomena on the other. The results of research using mathematical models, and supported by figures, and arithmetic and geometric sequences, grew in abundance. The foundation of this was that those working in this field considered sensation to be a phenomenon which possesses duration and intensity, and they believed that it could be measured like other, similar phenomena.

In addition to this, clear psychological research developed as the field turned to analysis. It strongly criticised the approach that made modern human consciousness a standard for judging primitive consciousness. Thus, there was a need to break down all sensory

---

4 This is a somewhat clumsy description of the skin's thermoreceptors. The cold receptors would not perceive a wire heated with fire as cold. Pain, sensed by the skin's pain receptors, would be the more likely sensation in this scenario.

phenomena which had been thought of as elementary but which, in fact, could be broken down into numerous elements.[5] Furthermore, sensory perception is more complicated than sensation. The analysis of perception is done either by the empirical method or by that of psychological analysis. The former is achieved by affecting a change in the conditions affecting perception and then observing what happens to it, thereby uncovering the elements of which it is composed, while the latter operates on the grounds that habit and the association of thoughts are composed of elementary cognitions, and that we gradually form a complex of these through habituation until we imagine that the system is simplistic, or not even a system at all. In this way, many phenomena have been reduced to their basic elements, such as spatial perception, for example.

With regard to critique of knowledge, Spencer returned to factualism and acknowledged the reality of existence. He didn't want to pursue the lengthy, complicated hypotheses of metaphysics. To Spencer, sentience and movement are proof of the reality of existence. However, this does not mean that the senses convey things to us as they are. Suffice it to say that there can be no experience of sensation in the psyche without that which it encounters in the external world existing. This was the view of Hermann von Helmholtz who said that the senses transform vibrations into sounds and colours by a magical power.

In the modern era it can be observed that the mathematical laws, which demonstrate the fixed relationships between sensory perception and its natural antecedents, such as the Weber-Fechner law,[6] challenged positions that had been previously held. Research now

---

5 The last word of this sentence 't-y/ī-n' ("تين") – the quotations marks are Mahfouz' – is a somewhat abrupt insertion and has not been included in the translation. It may be an attribution to the French positivist Hippolyte Taine (1828–1893), but this is not entirely clear. Mahfouz, Naguib, Ḥawla l-Adab wa-l-Falsafa, Cairo, 2003, p. 127

6 The original Arabic (قانونا فشزووبر) appears to be in error but is probably meant to signify the Weber-Fechner law. This law pertains to perception, combining the work of Ernst Heinrich Weber (1795–1878) and that of Gustav Fechner (1801–1887). Mahfouz, Naguib, Ḥawla l-Adab wa-l-Falsafa, Cairo, 2003, p. 128

turned its attention to studying the quality of sensations (*la qualité*) after having neglected to measure this.[7] The most important aspect of this that should be mentioned here was the discovery of new senses, through breaking down the five senses into more simple elements. It was found, for example, that touch comprises a special sensory organ for pressure, resistance, softness, hardness, dryness, and wetness. Furthermore, it possesses a sensory organ that specifically senses hotness and coldness; there are points on the skin which only sense heat and others which only sense coldness. These findings derive from the discoveries Magnus Blix, and the experiments of Alfred Goldscheider and Maximilian von Frey. Hermann Ebbinghaus advocated the existence of a special sense for pain which possesses special sensory nerves.[8] Furthermore, it was also observed that the sense of touch is related to the experience of love and affection as can be seen in the pleasure people derive from touching one another. In the year 1870 Brown discovered two senses in the ear: one for hearing and another for movement and balance.[9] In the year 1900 Henri Parinaud and Johannes von Kries discovered two senses in the eye: one that perceives white and black, and another that perceives the solar spectrum.[10]

With regard to sensory perception a novel, new theory was found to explain it: gestaltism. The first proponent of this was Christian von

---

7 The French term appears here as it does in the original essay (although the brackets and italics are mine). It corresponds to *kayfīya* in the original Arabic, translated here as 'the quality'. Mahfouz, Naguib, *Ḥawla l-Adab wa-l-Falsafa*, Cairo, 2003, p. 128

8 Mahfouz refers to a second person in this sentence, who, along with Ebbinghaus, advocated the opinion stated; however, I cannot identify to whom Mahfouz is referring with the original Arabic *y-w/ū-t-y/ī-k-w/ū* (يوتيكو) and have omitted the name from the translation. Mahfouz, Naguib, *Ḥawla l-Adab wa-l-Falsafa*, Cairo, 2003, p. 129

9 Mahfouz does not provide a forename here, simply the surname 'Brown' (برون), or one of its variants. One possibility is that it refers to Alexander Crum Brown (1838–1932) who theorised about the sense of balance in relation to the workings of the inner ear. Mahfouz, Naguib, *Ḥawla l-Adab wa-l-Falsafa*, Cairo, 2003, p. 129

10 Mahfouz probably means 'visible spectrum' rather than 'solar spectrum' (*bi-l-ṭayf al-shamsī*). Mahfouz, Naguib, *Ḥawla l-Adab wa-l-Falsafa*, Cairo, 2003, p. 129

Ehrenfels, and among its advocates were Max Wertheimer, Kurt Koffka, and Wolfgang Köhler. The significance of gestaltism is its claim that cognition does not begin with partial perceptions; rather, it begins with a general impression of things and perceptions as a result of analysis. Thus, if we are shown a drawing which is composed of a number of dots we cannot help but see it as an image of something, such as line or a circle. It represents a natural composition which the mind spontaneously assembles.

This is not the place to discuss Bergson's theory, which goes beyond the limits of psychology and, on the whole, returns to the factual approach. It suffices to say that, to Bergson, the brain does not create forms but receives them, and chooses from them that which will benefit practical life; the brain is an instrument of selection and activation.

Consciousness[1]

Consciousness, in the field of psychology, signifies the mind's cognizance of itself, and it almost amounts to an essential precondition for any psychological state. Because it is so closely connected to most phenomena, and because all people are habituated to it, our ancestors did not pay attention to it. This is because matters which are taken for granted must reach a state of fruition before anyone pays attention to them.

The natural philosophers did not turn their attention to investigating thought but pursued the study of external nature. They weren't sceptical about the capability of the mind, but they were not fully certain about it either. Later they began to turn their attention to the soul, indicated by the fact that they made a distinction between the spirit and matter. They spoke of this world as having a universal sentience. This conception of existence reveals that they were alert to the consciousness of the soul and its properties. We find a clear illustration of this among the Sophists because they believed in the existence of the rational mind and they examined it from numerous angles. Moreover, they made it a basis for knowing; they advocated the view that knowledge is relative, claiming that it depended upon the knower.

This evolution toward the knowledge of consciousness was crowned by Socrates who said, 'Know thyself'. Through this knowledge he wanted to discover the principles of logic and ethics. Plato turned his attention to the phenomenon of consciousness; however, his touching

---

1 Article from *al-Majalla al-Jadida* June 1935

on this was incidental in that it came about through his study concerning opposing sensations. He did not refer to consciousness by a particular appellation, nor did he devote one of his philosophical discourses to it. However, Plato got close to the modern meaning of consciousness when he drew a distinction between two types of sensations: those that do not pass beyond the sphere of the bodily organs, and those which advance further to reach the psyche. The principle behind this distinction is the notion that we are not conscious of the former type, but that we are conscious of the latter type.

Like Plato, Aristotle neither gave consciousness a name nor engaged it as a specific topic. However, he did provide a description of it in his study of the mind and the senses. From his views we can deduce that he did not conceive of consciousness as being a specific faculty which is independent; rather, he saw it as being connected to phenomena. When the eye sees, for example, it senses that it is seeing, and when the mind makes contact with a subject matter it knows that it is thinking, and so forth.

It was the Stoics who gave consciousness its conventional name, which came to be adopted within the fields of philosophy and psychology. They defined it as a sense through which the psyche knows itself. Since they believed that all truths were physical, they conceived of it as a sense of touch whose subject matter is internal. Furthermore, they also ascribed to it an important function in terms of knowing. That is to say, they believed that knowledge is a psychological process involving the digestion of things which pertain to the mind. We are not able to reach a degree of certainty concerning what we know; however, if we direct our consciousness toward this process and reassure ourselves of its soundness then the certainty of consciousness becomes a basis for every practical certainty.

In the mysticism of Neo-Platonism it is almost as though consciousness is something secondary. Neo-Platonists claim that the soul knows itself. They explain this through the idea that that the human soul is connected to both the soul of the world and the mind of the world, having originally descended from these. The mind knows itself, and the human soul acquired this characteristic from it. Consciousness enables the soul to perceive itself but it does not exalt it to the knowledge of God despite the link between them being intact. But why is this? The answer to this is that the soul is shackled to the body and the phantasm emits consciousness. Thus, the only path to God is through ridding oneself of the illusions of consciousness, the senses, and the body, and by practicing virtue. Knowledge of God is annihilation in him, insofar as consciousness ceases to exist through this.

This understanding is certainly a mystical one, because a mystic finds delight in annihilation in God and by forgetting his self, his sensations and desires. The philosophers believed that consciousness possessed another value in that it represents direct experience of the world of the soul. It also became a pillar of certitude under which Descartes found refuge after a long period of confusion during which he was plagued by doubts. Questioning everything – whether within his self or outside it – represented the starting point of his philosophy. However, the enormous doubt he experienced made him realise an important truth: he had doubts, and he could be in no doubt that he had doubts. This doubt meant that he was thinking, and since the thinker must think, therefore, he exists. Descartes' consciousness of doubt, or thought, is what led him to certitude and enabled him to construct his philosophy. He did not view consciousness as being a special faculty dedicated to a particular task; instead, he viewed it as being inseparable from the sum of mental processes. This is what is intuitively understood from there being a consciousness of thinking, because Descartes believed that thinking is the essence of the soul. The will, perception, and emotions come from thinking, and the person who is conscious of thinking is conscious of all of these.

It should also be mentioned here that Malebranche, who was a disciple of Descartes, did not hold the same opinion of consciousness as his teacher. This is because he viewed it as being closer to feeling than to knowledge. To Malebranche, consciousness allows us to perceive the soul, but we cannot perceive clearly. He does not deny the certainty of consciousness but argues that it is concealed.

It was through Leibniz that consciousness regained its position in philosophy because, ultimately, it formed the foundation of his philosophy. When he became convinced that the true nature of being boils down to the nature of the essences, or atoms, he found that these essences were forces, and that the soul too is a force. He examined the mind and discovered in it the truths of the atoms which make up being; this led him to believe in the importance of consciousness. His work was not limited to discovering the phenomena of the soul, however; he went beyond this in order to know the underlying essences of the phenomena.

Leibniz studied the matter of the subconscious mind. He said that there are an infinite number of feelings that we have no conscious awareness of. This is due either to their subtlety and their proliferation – inasmuch as this makes it impossible to distinguish between them – or due to their merging together to the extent that we cannot recognise them individually. This provides us with an explanation for the lack of conscious awareness caused by habit and familiarity, but also for the mystery of various sensations which reoccur, such as sorrowful and joyful psychological states which alternately affect us without our being able to explain them.

The importance of the role of consciousness endured in the philosophy of Locke. He considered experience to be the origin of all knowledge and believed that sensory perception is derived from it. It is sensory perception which conveys to us impressions of the internal world – involving internal contemplation, or consciousness – and those of the external world. All of our thoughts are the product of sensory perception and consciousness; however, some thoughts come together to form complex ideas, such as concepts of causality or duration. Consciousness is not enough to form these; rather, in this instance the task of both consciousness and perception is to put forth simple thoughts from which the psyche constructs something more complex. Consequently, consciousness does not know the essences of things. This was the opinion of another philosopher of the English school of empiricism: David Hume.[2] He was of the opinion that consciousness knows only the phenomena of the mind. As for that which we refer to

---

2 David Hume (1711–1776) was Scottish, not English.

as intellectual truths – such as cause and nature – these are illusions produced by the association of thoughts and meanings.

So far we have seen that there is a group of philosophers who view consciousness as a sense for perceiving the truth of the psyche and its essence, and another group who believe that the power of consciousness is limited to knowing the phenomena of the mind, that there is nothing within us except continuous phenomena, and that all substances of things are illusions. The critical philosophy of Kant attempted to reconcile these two conflicting philosophies. Consciousness does not know the soul in its essence, according to Kant; rather, it knows only phenomena. The soul really exists, but we can only know it insofar as it manifests itself to us. He did not reject the notion of the existence of essences but he did not claim that he was able to know them as they really are. Furthermore, he did not deny the existence of phenomena, but neither did he say that they were the only things which exist.

But why is it that truths appear to us other than they are? This is because the sensory perceptions which convey impressions of the world to us are connected together and transformed into knowledge through rational principles. The rational mind participates in forming truths. Therefore, in the end we do not comprehend them as they are, but as they are revealed to us by rational principles. Consciousness is influenced by the mind because it only perceives the truths of the soul after the mind has conceived of them by means of its principles. However, there are two types of consciousness: experiential consciousness, which is associated with the phenomena of the psyche prior to their being affected by the rational mind; and theoretical consciousness, which is associated with the rational mind when it brings together the phenomena of the psyche and the external world.

Kant also directed his attention to the subconscious mind. He believed that it was occupied with the major part of psychological life. The telescope, for example, reveals to us thousands of celestial bodies that the naked eye cannot perceive.

Among the adherents of the Scottish school was someone who conceived of consciousness in a new way. Until now we have not

encountered him among the philosophers who considered consciousness to be a distinct faculty which observes our internal life without
participating in it. I am speaking of Reid who said that we are aware of
our thoughts and all of the processes of our mind through a faculty that
we refer to as 'consciousness'. Consciousness is cognizant of the phenomena but not of the psyche in its essence. He responded to Hume's
claim that there is nothing more abstruse than notions of potentiality,
and causation, and so forth, by saying that we necessarily come to
comprehend as a result of our being conscious of our minds, for we
are conscious of the psychological processes which inspire concepts
of potentiality, and others.

However, there was someone among Scottish philosophers who
disagreed with Reid's take on consciousness: Sir William Hamilton. He
was of the opinion that it is not a separate faculty and that it is not dis-
tinguishable from the states which it is conscious of. He characterised
it as a general state that applied to all of the psychological processes
which increase the level of potential. Hamilton also observed that the
sphere of consciousness could not be confined to states which are
purely mental in nature; this is because consciousness extends to the
sphere of the faculties of the psyche. When we perceive the world by
means of our faculties, and discern one of its truths, we are also conscious of it. Furthermore, our consciousness spreads to the external
world.

Hamilton recognised the existence of the subconscious mind; certain
signs informed him of this view. The greatest treasures of the intellect –
such as language and science – can often remain beyond the sphere of
consciousness. Those who suffer certain mental illnesses, for example,
sometimes rave about things that they can have no prior knowledge of.
Furthermore, with regard to the association of meanings, there are subconscious connections which require careful examination to unravel.

Concerning the era of the modern, empirical school of thought –
which was represented by Stuart Mill, Bain and Spencer, and which
was actually an extension of the old, empirical school that Locke and
Hume had given rise to – I will say this: during this era consciousness
came to be viewed in a new way and Darwin's scientific theory of

evolution had a significant part in this. It was understood that the new notion of consciousness could not be an exact copy of the old one. Furthermore, the illusions of consciousness came to be understood. For example, consciousness acquaints us with psychological phenomena and makes us believe that they are simplistic but, in truth, they are complex. It is possible to break them down into the many different elements which have been slowly formed over the passage of time and which are subject to the laws of evolution.

According to this school of thought, consciousness only perceives phenomena. This is consistent with scientific psychology which seeks only to connect the phenomena with principles and uncover the circumstances around their association. Mill rejected the existence of a subconscious mind. Concerning influencing factors that we do not sense, he said that these are physiological. The meaning here is that the potentiality of these influencing factors does not reach the nerve centres and they are not picked up by the senses. The absence of awareness in this case is not psychological but pertains to the nervous system.

To Spencer consciousness had to be explained by movement and change. The existence of a certain psychological state does not produce consciousness of it; rather, consciousness occurs when a change from one state changes to another takes place. It is important to mention here that much thought has been directed toward the phenomena of the subconscious, and its remarkable phenomena have been described at length. Some, however, have gone too far – such as Henry Maudsley, for example – and claimed that consciousness itself is something secondary.

If we now move toward the modern period we find three theories concerning consciousness that were put forth by three of its distinguished thinkers: William James, Bergson and Hamelin. James' method of thinking proceeded from something complex to something simple. He tried to find out about psychological states on the basis of his knowledge of the mind, rather than find out about the mind by comparing psychological states and mentally examining them.

Conscious is the foremost psychological phenomenon and all psychological states are linked to it. However, consciousness does not exist outside the different states, and states that are separate from it do not exist. Consciousness is the backbone of psychological states; it joins them together and, from them, creates a totality that is indivisible. It does, however, pertain to the individual; that is to say, the consciousness of one individual is separate from that of other individuals.

Psychological states continually undergo renewal and change. When we experience a psychological state twice, there will be a change in the second instance that will make it different in nature from the first instance. Consciousness is continuous like a flowing stream. As with a stream, the surface is not the same as the depths. There is a state within consciousness where thought ceases activity, and another in which thought swims. Undoubtedly it is easy to observe and describe first state; for this reason the major part of attention is directed towards it. But we must not neglect the second state: the state of activity. Consciousness perceives these two states simultaneously; that is, it perceives the phenomena of the mind and the relationships between them. This means that consciousness is compositional. It does not forget the whole as it breaks down the components, and it sustains its continuity despite interrupting the phenomenon.

Consciousness does not take a neutral stance toward the different psychological states: it is partial toward some while it neglects others. It is said that the states to which consciousness inclines are in the centre while those which it turns away from are at the margin, and all of the states turn between the centre and the margin according to the psychological conditions. This is what produces the stream and it explains why some states have ascendancy over others, being of more practical concern in the life of the individual. Bergson followed the same approach. The first thing he noticed was that consciousness is not limited to the present because it has a memory of the past and it can envision the future. What we perceive is really a scale of psychological time which links our immediate past and near future. Or to put it another way, consciousness is a bridge between the past and the future. But what is the utility of this bridge?

The philosophy of Bergson responds to this question as follows: consciousness appears when life does, accompanying it like a shadow.

This is because it is the basis of action; it is through it that matters are planned and a decision is taken. It is fully capable of this due to its memory of the past and its ability to make predictions about the future. Because of all of this it is able to focus and cope whenever the living being encounters circumstances which require direction and making a choice between manifold options. However, it becomes weak when it can dispense with having to make choices, acting mechanically or on the basis of habit. Since choice is synonymous with freedom, the work of consciousness is based on freedom and, thus, it governs freedom in actuality. Thus, the role of consciousness is concerned with memory, assessing the future, choice, and freedom.

But what is the nature of consciousness? Bergson's answer to this question is sublime and mystical. He was not satisfied with the stance of empirical science. He said, for example, that consciousness cannot be broken down into distinct, separate, independent states, but that consciousness is a continuous union, like a musical tone. We are to envisage a musical tone that is aware of itself and forms itself. This is how we should understand consciousness.

We express the nature of consciousness through language and rational analysis, but all of this distorts its nature and presents us with something other than what it is. Consciousness is a unity in terms of form, but in terms of essence it is a pure attribute, i.e., it is not a quantity. This was Bergson's response to those who claimed that they were measuring the phenomena of consciousness as material phenomena. He attributed this notion to the commonly-held view that the strongest emotion is greater in terms of quantity than other emotions. This is a critique is based upon inner contemplation and represents an attempt to establish psychology on new grounds by cleansing the mind of common illusions and the borrowings of natural psychology.

As for Hamelin, he did not distinguish consciousness from thought. Since, in his view, consciousness comprises the reality of existence, nothing is outside the sphere of consciousness whether it pertains to the self of man or to external existence. He did not see the mind as having two parts, i.e., one which is conscious and another which is the subject of the former. To him, these two parts were a single entity that is conscious of itself. However, if we say that all phenomena are the phenomena of consciousness then how can we distinguish psychological phenomena from other types of phenomena? Were we to say that they do not extend to, or that they do not come under, sensory perception, then we define them negatively. In fact, the most important thing that differentiates them is that they are subjective. That is to say, we have a strong feeling that we are the active agent in their existence and their fashioning. Like Bergson, Hamelin viewed consciousness as having the task of making choices. Thus, also like Bergson, he saw freedom as a prerequisite in relation to its existence.

There are now theories for the subconscious just as there are for consciousness. There are two ways of conceiving of it: one way is to consider it as a state of consciousness, and the other is to view it as a second consciousness which is independent, like another self-existent mind. In the first instance it is one phenomenon among the other psychological phenomena, and in the second instance it is an existing entity – another living entity inside the human being. We can see an illustration of the first case in the way people mechanically write down something that is being dictated to them without being aware of what they are doing. With regard to the second case, an example of it is found in the medium who performs wonders through hypnosis or through what is known as a séance. The theories that state that the subconscious mind is something distinct and hidden are built upon the reality of multiple personalities. Among those associated with this view is Freud. He viewed the libido as a personality living within the human being and which is in a continuous struggle with another personality: the social personality. Though the former is suppressed by the latter in actual life, it is set free in dreams.

The theories which argue that the subconscious is a phenomenon vary. Among them we find the belief that all psychological phenomena are liable to sink below the surface of the subconscious; it makes no difference whether these phenomena are sublime thoughts or baser appetites connected to the senses. Sometimes there is an instrument involved in thinking, just as there is in actions. Furthermore, the subconscious mind is present behind the most brilliant gifts, such as those

of invention, inspiration, and genius. Indeed, the creative act itself –
that is, the essential, mental work – is subconscious.

Among the others, however, there is a theory that restricts the sphere
of the subconscious to feeling, excluding it from the thinking process.
Ribot stated that if there is a subconscious, then it exists in a state of
longing that is antecedent to consciousness.

We can conclude the subject by summarising the theories of consciousness as follows:

1. There is the theory held by some thinkers of the Scottish
   Enlightenment which argues that consciousness is an attribute that is distinct from psychological phenomena. This idea,
   however, has fallen out of favour.
2. There is that of the empirical school; they tried to make psychology a science that solely studies psychological phenomena. According to this school of thought, consciousness is
   an attribute that connects physiological phenomena when a
   certain level of potential is reached.
3. There is the theory associated with the Kantian, critical school.
   This school of thought holds the view that consciousness does
   not reveal the essence of the psyche to us; rather, we see it only
   as it appears to us.
4. There is the spiritual theory. Proponents of this believe that
   consciousness breaks through to the essence, the truth, and
   the absolute. This theory brings psychology into the realm of
   metaphysics.

Theories of the Mind[1]

The issue of the mind is an issue of knowledge, and it is based on this question: does the mind receive knowledge without having any control over it, or, is it an active agent that possesses its own creative being which is independent of experience?

The first signs of this theory appeared when early philosophers made a distinction between that which is apprehended by the rational faculty and that which is perceived by the senses, and when some of them explained the ignorance of people as being due to their abandoning themselves to the senses and the consequences that this occasions. Heraclitus stated that wisdom is knowledge of the mind; he believed that the essence of the mind was not separate from the essence of being, which he considered to be primordial fire. This induced early philosophers to hold the senses in contempt. Their theories about existence and its origin were metaphysical, and not based on sensory evidence, which they held in low regard.

When Socrates came along he stated that truth is innate within the human being, the proof of this being that by reflecting on our thoughts and actions our ignorance is revealed to us; this knowledge of ignorance then leads us to the existence of truth within us. Accordingly, without this, it would be impossible for us to judge anything as being ignorance and error, because judgment requires that we have a concept of truth and knowledge. The means of discovering this knowledge is through self-reflection, and by the aid of the processes of induction, definition, and deduction.

---

1 Article from *al-Majalla al-Jadida* July 1935

Plato followed the method of his teacher, but he believed that recollection was the key to true knowledge. This is because he believed
that man, prior to his descent to this existence, had lived in an ideal
world and that he retained the primary truths while occupying this
lower existence. These truths, however, are in a state of slumber, but
wakefulness returns to them if the person examines the world which is
perceptible through the senses. This examination of his led to the recollection of the primary truths. Thus, knowledge is recollection.

Aristotle agreed with Plato and Socrates with regard to their view
that the subject of knowledge is the essence, or the nature, of the
thing. Aristotle, however, gave a more extensive explanation. He said
that the mind is two minds: the passive mind and the active, or operative, mind – a duality that corresponds to nature. In nature there is
substance which can take any form, and there is the active cause
which determines this form. With regard to the passive mind, this is
the matter of thought, it is always connected to experience and sensation, depends on induction in the extraction of general ideas, and
on deduction by analogy in drawing conclusions from these ideas.
However, these processes require rational principles that act to regu-
late them and lead to certitude, because knowledge is not based on
experience alone. These principles know by means of intuition, and
the agent of this intuition is the operative mind. The operative mind
is that which interprets those things which are sensed by the passive
mind. Without it there can be no intellectual truth and knowledge
would be impossible to attain.

The philosophies of Stoicism and Epicureanism are considered to
be the starting point for experiential philosophy. Stoicism highlighted
the role of the will in thinking and in the formation of knowledge.
Epicureanism, on the other hand, made sensory perception the foundation of all knowledge. Then came Neo-Platonism and the Christian
philosophies which, on the whole, did not produce anything new in
the world of thought, but lived indebted to the ancient philosophies.
At that time, knowledge consisted of searching for a fixed essence
within changing events that would communicate knowledge of God,
this being the desired outcome.

The course of knowledge changed in the 16th century when Descartes made the rational mind a force for truth and knowledge.[2] In fact, his work picked up from Plato; this is because the philosophers of this century had a low opinion of the medieval philosophy and no longer had faith in its grand loftiness. They sought liberation from its chains in rational scepticism, so, naturally, they sought clarity in their philosophies. Descartes found in mathematics a perfect model for clear and indisputable science. He wanted the philosophical method – which at that time focussed on God, the soul, and nature – to be based upon the mathematical model. Accordingly, the rational mind would move from the simple to the complex; from certain, self-evident, rational principles to complex phenomena. Here, intuition reveals rational principles, mental connections are made through these principles, knowledge is constructed from them, and the activity of thought – which produces them – is the logical conclusion. The mind is that which constructs the edifice of knowledge by revealing its principles and making connections between them.

Descartes believed that there were simple, clear, evident concepts in the mind that we can know through intuition and introspection. Now, if we become aware of these, then, through them, we have the ability to infer knowledge concerning the soul and nature. The concepts included ideas such as 'the soul', 'extensity', and others. One might address objection to Descartes saying: you hold the opinion that concepts such as 'the soul' and 'extensity' are clear and simple, that their existence is innate within the mind, and that intuition is enough to reveal them. But it seems that you may deduce from these concepts whatever you desire, imagining that you have produced knowledge. According to you, the concept of 'the soul' designates a real soul within the human being, and the concept of 'extensity' designates an established essence that is discernible through perceptible phenomena. But who informed you that these concepts correspond to truths in actual existence? What's there to prevent anyone from saying that all of these

2 Mahfouz probably means the 17th century here; Descartes was still an infant at the close of the 16th century, being born in 1596.

concepts are nothing more than the illusions of a mind that have been created by thinking itself?

In reality, Descartes didn't establish any proof that actually verified these concepts. He did rationalise their truth, however; he said that the inference in doubting the truth of these concepts is that God deceives us and casts our minds into error. This is because it is he who created our minds and he makes our minds believe that their perceived thoughts are true in reality. Thus, if this were true, then God would be a deceiver. But, since God is true and deemed to above such a thing, and since it is not possible to raise doubt to the status of truth, then our belief in our thoughts is true. Thus, God guarantees scientific certainty and is triumphant over the doubt which is repeatedly attacked by rationalism.[3]

This rational, or mathematical, approach which was advocated by Descartes was taken up by the Cartesian school of thought. Two of its most outstanding philosophers were Malebranche and Spinoza. Locke, the English philosopher, vehemently opposed the Cartesian school of thought. To Descartes, mathematics was an example of scientific certainty, and deduction was a true method. With regard to Locke, however, he did not see here a model of natural science, nor of inductive method. He attacked Descartes' ideas about innate ideas and rational principles saying that they could not possibly be inborn. His evidence was that children and savages could not comprehend their meaning, but that comprehension requires learning and effort in order that their meanings can be mentally explored.

To Locke, the mind was a blank slate. He stated that it is experience and the senses that fill this slate with images and meanings, and that the mind is endowed with the ability to discriminate and to synthesise. From simple thoughts it is able to form universal concepts. Analysis and synthesis can explain the mode of forming those ideas which Descartes viewed as innate. He explained, for example, the idea of 'God' as coming from man's observation of his psyche and its

---

3 This appears to be a discussion of the Cartesian idea of the 'deceptive god', often associated with that of the 'evil demon'.

properties. Furthermore, these capabilities conceive of God through infinite stages of power and perfection, ending up at the conception of a perfect being. And perhaps a person imagines, just as Descartes did, that their idea is simple and innate, and that it has been revealed by mental intuition. It is through experience, however, both external and internal, that our minds form all of the ideas that inside them.

Leibniz tried to reconcile these two philosophies. Like Descartes, his leaning was mathematical; however, he wanted to expand the horizons of the mind and diversify his methods. He agreed with Locke in his critique concerning Descartes' philosophy of innate ideas; the fact that children and savages are ignorant of these ideas led him to doubt that they existed innately in man. On the other hand, however, he perceived that experience and observation were not enough to explain all of the rational truths. Experience, for example, pertains to the individual: it is relative. However, there are universal, necessary truths whose antitheses the mind cannot conceive of. Innate principles exist but they do not make themselves known to the conscious mind in every instance; rather, experience is required in order to make them known truths so that their potential is actualised in the mind. Truths are of two types: those that are innate, and those that come through experience or facts. The first are necessary and universal, like $2 + 2 = 4$, for example. The second are those which are known by the senses or by the conscious mind, such as historical fact.

With regard to David Hume, he carried on the philosophy of Locke. Hume attributed all knowledge to external and internal experience, and he completely rejected the notion of necessary ideas. Furthermore, he expanded upon Locke's philosophy saying that the mind does not possess an effective power or capability to synthesise and analyse, but that, on the whole, it is subject to laws which act freely within it, just as natural laws act freely within nature. Thus, the psychological system is conceived of in light of a model of nature's system; it assumes the existence of laws which control the psychological realm, just as the law of gravitation has power over phenomena in nature. These psychological laws are laws of association and correlation. It is these which make all of the sensory perceptions, imaginations, and feelings into a working system which, through its order, makes us believe that it relies on innate and necessary principles that God has engraved within us. The laws of correlation are likeness and connection in time, space, and causality. On the basis of this, Hume explains the law of causality by saying that its significance is that when we observe specific premises we expect specific outcomes. So where do we get this expectation from? Does it come from the nature of things? Not at all, it is because, in reality, we see only consecutive phenomena. Furthermore, we do not observe a necessary force which makes the antecedent a determining cause that occasions what follows. So where do we get this belief? We get it from the laws of correlation and habit. We see two consecutive events which we connect to causality – always they go together. It is a connection in time and space, subsequently we always see the same premises and the same outcomes: this is similarity. Through successive repetition, habit is formed and we come to anticipate its effect, and through the action of the aforementioned laws we can deduce determined outcomes when specific premises are manifest to us. To summarise, it can be said that the mind's function here is limited to receiving various sensory perceptions and feelings, as well as sensitivity towards the laws of correlation.

Kant encountered these philosophies but he was not convinced by their claims with regard to metaphysics nor of the physiology of the mind, as conceived by Locke and Hume. He addressed the matter, which had become increasingly disputed among the rationalists and the empiricists, with this question: is rational, a priori knowledge – that is, knowledge which is independent of experience – possible? He responds to this question in the affirmative, distinguishing three types:

1. Mathematics.
2. Principles of natural science.
3. Metaphysics (at least in the opinion of those who believe in metaphysics).

He believed that the mind conceived of things within the limits of its nature, and evaluated them according to its natural modes, or forms.

However, these modes are only employed by the mind when experience presents it with the substance of knowledge.

From this it is clear to us that he made a distinction between two things in knowledge: the substance of knowledge, that which is conveyed to it by the senses; and the form of knowledge, this is that which the mind attaches to the former. Experiential knowledge is the mixing of substance with form, or the substance as seen by the mind through its forms. This is the novel position taken by Kant. He wanted to propose that the perception of things does not present the things to us as they are in their essence, but this does not mean that they are merely illusions and images which do not extend beyond the limits of the mind.

Kant presents existence to us through the forms of the mind. He gives us existence as something that we can conceive of in accordance with the capacity of rational principles. In light of this he differed from the adherents of idealism. Furthermore, to Kant, mental forms differed from the notion of innate ideas held by Descartes and Leibniz. To the Cartesian school of thought, the mind has the ability to comprehend essences, such as those of God and the soul. Mental forms, however – that is to say, the principles of the mind, in general – do not have a particular subject matter; rather, all phenomena that we encounter are subject to them and connected due to them.

Kant spoke of three levels of knowing: that which the senses convey, which is the subject matter, or the phenomena; the experiential mind, which creates the principles and forms for connecting phenomena; and the abstract mind, which has, at its core, a tendency towards oneness. The abstract mind goes beyond the limits of experience and creates issues that cannot be resolved. Kant then sets out to present an exposition on the mental forms and prove that the mind is incapable of attaining the absolute, or knowledge concerning the essences of things.

After Kant, the elemental truths were described as being universal and necessary. This can be attributed, as we know, to them being forms of the mind. They cannot to be conceived of as other. Were they a result of experience, then it would be impossible to accord them the characteristics of universality and necessity. This is because experience presents us with a particular set of circumstance within a particular time. With regard to establishing a rule for all circumstances and all instances, this is determined by the mind and not by experience. However, the English empirical school of thought, which was the successor of Hume's philosophy, did not yield to this explanation, though they acknowledged a general conviction that regarded these universal, necessary truths as being true. John Stuart Mill drew on psychology to explain them. Concerning necessity, he said that if two thoughts exist together, or consecutively, then one invokes the other according to the rule of the association of meanings. Thus, when two thoughts are always present together, they become linked in the mind and we imagine – because of their perpetual connection – the existence of a necessary relationship between them. With regard to the prevalence of these truths among everyone, this can be attributed to the nature of human beings themselves, in that they are driven toward certain experiences from which result conceptions of the principal truths. Therefore, the fundamental truths are not innate mental forms: they are merely the effects of experience which are subject to the law of association, and which have been established by repetition over time.

Spencer was one of the men belonging to this school of thought. In explaining the mind, and its main principles, he relied upon the theory of evolution and of hereditary transmission, and sought answers in physiology. He did not fundamentally differ from Mill, because, like him, he viewed habit and association as the basis for the formation of mental forms. However, he stated that individual experience is not enough. He replaced this notion with one involving the experience of species as resulting from hereditary transmission. Psychological states, which are interconnected, and which frequently coincide together, form a general inclination which can be inherited. This moves toward becoming fully embedded, taking its final form in mental principles.

A clearer explanation of hereditary transmission given by Spencer is that psychological life corresponds to corporeal life and influences it, inasmuch as each psychological state has its equivalent in the neurological system. The linking together of two thoughts, for example, involves an interlocking within the brain, and in this way – over the passage of generations – mental principles are formed which he believed to be inborn. According to this view these principles are a result of the effects of inherited experience; however, since experiences are liable to change, mental principles are not final as some believe. This justifies Spencer's view of the mind because, according to him, there is a correspondence which always moves toward consummation between the mind and nature.

In the manner of Kant, critics of the mind appeared in the modern era whose goal was to define its principles and describe them. However, they disagreed with Kant in their conceptualisation of the mind. Kant had viewed it as a special faculty which is distinct from the senses. The modern critics, Charles Bernard Renouvier, Octave Hamelin, and Lange,[4] however, expanded its signification until it came to include sensory perception and the will. These critics were united in having the same goal of arranging the principles of the mind into categories, though they differed in terms of their respective approaches. Renouvier and Lange relied on experience in determining these principles, while Hamelin applied himself to mental analysis. Durkheim similarly saw the mind as a set of principles to which human beings are subject to in how they conceive of things. However, he believed that it is not enough that we know what these principles are and how they are connected; rather, we need to arrive at their sources. To Durkheim, these sources are in the collective society.

Durkheim opposed those of the opinion that people come together because their minds lead them to value the benefits of community life. Instead, he believed that the mind itself is fashioned by the collective society. Man is social; he develops through learning the ideas of the community, and by adopting its manners and ways of thinking. If he pays attention to himself and observes his mind he will find principles

---

4 It is unclear to whom the third name of this trio refers. The Arabic *l-y/ī-n-kh* (لينخ) provides no forename and may well be a misspelling. If error is involved in this case, one possibility is the German philosopher Friedrich Albert Lange (1828–1875) who is considered to be a member of the Neo-Kantian school of thought. I have taken the liberty of using the surname 'Lange' in the text. Mahfouz, Naguib, *Ḥawla l-Adab wa-l-Falsafa*, Cairo, 2003, p. 155

within it which he himself did not construct and which never formed part of his personal experience. Man readily accepts these principles as being natural and innate. For example, as a principle, mentality is governed by religious belief or religion, which, according to Durkheim, is responsible for social phenomena. The prevalence of these principles among diverse and separated peoples is attributable to similarities in the nature of collective societies themselves – no matter where they happen to be – insofar as only one set of principles arise. Man is unable to conceive of other principles which are at variance with these. By this, Durkheim thought that he had reconciled the empiricists and the rationalists, for the mind is not the creation of an individual, nor is it an innate gift; rather, it is the product of society.

William James' theory concerning the mind is considered to be a return to empiricism. However, he did not reject the important role of rationality in knowing. To James, rationality complements sensory knowledge and puts it in order. Rational knowledge is enlightened sensory knowledge, and experience is a direct connection between the rational mind and truth. This does not mean that it attains perfection, for it is hindered insofar as experience fails to attain the level of perfection. In this, James differed from Bergson.

Bergson believed that perfect truth is impossible for the mind. This is because the mind alters the truth of experience, adapting it in order to expedite the actions of the person. To Bergson the mind is limited; its sphere is matter and its goal is action. It can hardly know anything unless it is in a state of calm and detachment. If it extends itself to trying to understand life, then its inadequacy becomes apparent. The means of fathoming the depths of life are intuition, or insight. This is the direct knowledge which merges us with the depths of life, making us experience its truth. This is the source of creative genius in art and ethics. Despite this, however, Bergson did not hold the mind in low esteem. He believed that if the mind acts jointly with intuition it attains knowledge of life or philosophy – alone, however, it can recognise neither knowledge nor matter.

Before concluding here, we should also highlight Léon Brunschvig's view of the mind. He had no faith in either the rationalists or the empiricists, nor did he envision the mind as a consummate system of principles. To Brunschvig the mind is not created fully formed; instead, it develops gradually. It determines principles and forms through its connection to experience. In this way it advances toward consummation in continual steps.

From this we can see that the issue of the mind began with the critique of sensory perception and evolved through the theories of Descartes, the criticism of Kant, and the empiricism of Mill. In the modern period some have conceived of the mind as a system of principles and tried to discover these, whether they sought these in the mind or in experience. Others ascribed it to collective society, while others still have spoken about it as something which fulfils a function in human life.

Language[1]

The celestial bodies in their orbits, the mind with its ideas, and life in its numerous manifestations are not more wondrous than those universal signs which are so commonplace that one forgets how miraculous they are. I am referring here to words, or language. The word is truly magical. It is the place the soul is hidden – emotions and thoughts slumber therein just as life slumbers in the heart. But what is language? What is the source of words? And what is their connection to the mind?

Generally speaking, language consists of signs which express thought – that is, inasmuch as it conveys emotions, desires, and ideas. Some of these signs are perceived through the sense of touch – the blind use Braille, for example – some are perceived through sight, and others are received by the ear. Among those signs which are heard are those which are syncopated, such as a scream, and those which are clear, such as speech.

There is a difference between studying the science of philology and the philosophy of language. The former is concerned with studying the evolution of language – its change, and the development of its structure. With regard to psychology, this studies the source of language and its relationship with thought.

Plato took up the issue of language in his dialogue *Cratylus* wherein he examined two opposing opinions on the matter. The first of these was that of Democritus; he viewed language as conventional and

---

1 Article from *al-Majalla al-Jadida* August 1935

its existence as arbitrary. There is nothing to prevent someone from altering the names of things however they please, or from applying whatever meaning they want to them. The second of these two opinions is that of Cratylus, who was a pupil of Heraclitus. He believed that there is a natural relationship between the designation and the thing designated. The designation expresses the nature of the thing insofar as whoever knows the designation also knows the thing itself. Thus, he believed that it was God who revealed to the first man the first words.

Plato criticised the former of these views saying that the actions of man are limited by the nature of things. You can only burn a substance if you possess the means required to set it alight. Furthermore, the word-maker is bound by the nature of things when he tries to create names for them. However, Plato didn't fully support Cratylus' idea either. He didn't believe that if someone knows the names of things then he also knows the truth of things, nor did he accept that words are attributable to a divine source. After all, how can words derive from a divine source if they are not free from defects and flaws? Thus, to Plato, words don't express the natures of things, even though they are similar to these natures. Furthermore, these natures possess that which a designation cannot convey. Thus, convention and arbitrariness inevitably play a role in the construction of language. Plato believed that in order to apply a name to something, you first have to know what it is. Thus, thought is prior to language.

Up until this point it should be noted that the examination of language was confined to the matter of its expression with regard to the essences of things. The Epicureans, however, took the subject in another direction; they saw it the context of history and the soul. They saw language, before all else, as being a sign of the soul. However, its existence and evolution are influenced by human requirements. Speech is a natural form of expression, because each human being possesses natural organs which they use without thinking – naturally and spontaneously. However, because every social community has feelings, ideas, and temperaments, which are particular to it, and since each language is an expression of all of these, languages differ according to different peoples. This is how different languages arise, and it signifies a process of modification in the formation of language. This process is very beneficial in relation to the defining of meanings, just as it helps the thinker to create particular words for comprehensive ideas and universal concepts. They are concepts which originate in thinking and contemplation, not as a revelation within the person.

To summarise this we can say that, with the exception of Cratylus, the ancient thinkers were in unanimous agreement that language is a human creation. With regards to words, there are those who said that they express the truths of things, and there are those who said that they are arbitrary in nature, then there is Epicurus who said that they give expression to states of the soul and bring language into being.

If we now turn to discuss the empirical school, which was headed by Locke, we will find that the study of language becomes a highly respected subject. This is because the empiricists saw that there was a strong relationship between the mind and language; indeed, Locke regarded it as futile to study the mind without first understanding language.

The faculty of speech is natural and it has its source within the organic apparatus. But this alone is not enough to produce language – otherwise parrots would have language. Language requires a rational capacity which associates mental concepts with verbal sounds. But even if this is sufficient to produce a language, it will remain a deficient one unless it is perfected through the formation of a comprehensive system of words which encompasses the signification of many things. It is the need to assign a name to each thing which eliminates confusion. From this it can be understood that even if the faculty of language is natural, expressions are formed arbitrarily and through convention. Nothing better demonstrates this than the multiplicity of languages, for if words conveyed the truths of things, then the multiplicity of different languages would not exist.

The cause behind speech is the need for people to communicate. It can be observed that language moves from the sensory to the intangible and from the specific to the general. Many abstract words are derived from sensory phenomena; the word 'soul', for example, is derived from sensory phenomena like 'breath'[2] Locke viewed them as being derived from things perceived by the senses, like the mind. There is no doubt that generic nouns – such as 'man', for example – came after proper nouns, such as 'Muhammad' or 'Ali'.

When Leibniz arrived, he responded to the view of the empiricists, opposing some aspects of it. Above all else he is known for founding the science of philology. He was concerned with the applying the comparative, scientific method to the study of language, claiming that significant findings would arise from this. To Liebniz, languages represented a more ancient sign of man's soul and his mind than arts and literature; by comparing them we are shown profound truths about man, about his mentality, and about shared human perception. As for Leibniz' response to the empirical school, he disagreed with the philosophy of Locke which contained these two points:

1. At first, words specifically signified individual things.
2. They are formed arbitrarily as a result of consensus.

To him, words did not originally signify individual things, because generic words are necessary in the formation of language. Indeed, it would be impossible for man to speak if he only had isolated words. Experience supports this; when children begin to learn language, for example, they frequently use generic words, such as 'animals', 'plants', or 'thing', rather than specific nouns which signify individual types of species. With regard to the second point, he did not unreservedly accept this, for language, though it may not be divine or innate, is not purely arbitrary and the causes for its existence may be innate or inborn. Furthermore, he noted that there are letters which convey force, such as the letter 'A', and others which convey delicacy, such as

---

2 In Arabic the word 'soul' or 'psyche' (nafs) resembles the word 'breath' (nafas) – both are derived from the same triliteral root (n-f-s). Mahfouz, Naguib, Hawla l-Adab wa-l-Falsafa, Cairo, 2003, p. 162

the letter 'D'.[3] This demonstrates the existence of a general relationship between things, sounds, and the movements of the vocal organs.

In the 18th century the interest of philosophers in determining the relationship between thought and language increased. Condillac went so far as to say that thought follows language, that an innate language exists even if it is not encountered by thoughts, and that knowledge itself is nothing more than a systematised language.

What is the source of language? The first form of language is the language of physical expression. Our outer appearance expresses our internal feelings. This language is neither voluntary nor arbitrary – it is natural. These expressive movements which exist alongside the emotions have no precedent with regard to the individual's endeavour to express his emotional states. The expressions of the body are a natural language existing in man prior to the desire to utilise them. His task is to discover them. However, the language of bodily expression only exists in the true sense when the signs express psychological states, and this is only achieved when man feels the need for mutual understanding, in order to achieve the benefit or gain that is brought about through mutual exchange.

The language of speech emerged after this. It began as a cry, following on from bodily movements and resembling them in terms of strength or feebleness. Later, it began to separate from them, little by little, until it became entirely independent. Its richness increased, with its way having been paved by the noises found in nature, the cries of the animals, and the abundant models to be copied and imitated. Language is inborn inasmuch as the organs of movement and the cry are also inborn. Man discovered how to use them when he felt the need for mutual understanding. The role of convention is to expand the sphere of language – nothing more.

Charles de Brosses accepted the theory of the 18th century philosophers which held that language develops from something poor and simple to something that is rich and developed. However, he viewed

---

3 Mahfouz uses modern Latin script for the letters here, not Arabic. Mahfouz, Naguib, Ḥawla l-Adab wa-l-Falsafa, Cairo, 2003, p. 163

language as a matter of necessity whose form is inevitably determined by the thing designated and the sound. Each thing affects the mind in a way which is particular to it. There is a natural link between the thing and its effect on the mind, just as there is a natural association between the given psychological effect and the sound which man applies to it in order to signify it. Language develops mechanically and its development is determined by the thing, on one hand, and the sound, on the other. This led him to believe that there is a single, primitive language. He was convinced of this idea, even though he had no scientific evidence to support it – and it has not been proven since.

We find in Rousseau the spirit of the 18th century, during which time language was considered to be natural. Rousseau disagreed with de Condillac with regard to his understanding of nature and the origin of primitive language. De Condillac had said that we find the cause for language in man's need. Rousseau, however, argued that emotions were what caused language, because need sows division among the people, making some the enemies of others. With regard to emotions – emotions such as love, hatred, and joy – these cause the first sounds to be made through people's mouths. Furthermore, according to Rousseau, the primitive language is not a precise language; rather, it is a poetic language which more closely resembles music than it does a language of precision – a designation which it would be unworthy of.

He opposed de Brosses' definition of language as being in the thing and the sound, for if that were true, then animals would possess language, since they have a connection to their environments and God has endowed them with the ability to produce sound. The truth, however, is that language has its source in a special faculty which uses sound to express things. Furthermore, he noted the influence of the environment with regard to the variegation of languages; some languages are gentle and delicate while others are strong and harsh, and so forth.

Among the philosophers of this period we find Louis Gabriel Ambroise de Bonald who returned to an ancient view of Cratylus. He claimed that the source of language is divine, for how could man be destined to create it? And if it were possible for him to create language, then how is it possible for him to teach it to others, since this can only be done if they possess a language which they mutually understand?

It was de Biran, however, who altered the trajectory of this matter. He no longer asked about the source of signs; it didn't matter to him if the source was divine, natural, or human. Signs only become a language in the true sense when human beings employ them to communicate their psychological states and if they express the meanings of these thereby. But how did this take place? The sign becomes language when its use is voluntary. Nature supplies children with signs so that they can communicate their needs, but this cannot be said to be language unless the child uses these signs with the intention of expression, as an act of will. If children feel pain, they scream. However, the scream does not amount to a language unless the child utilises it with intent – in the absence of any pain, for example – in order to have the wet nurse hasten to him and take him in her arms or feed him, and so forth. By acting in this way the child reveals his humanness and this is how true language is formed.

More recently there have been significant advances the field of linguistic philosophy which can be traced to the progress of comparative philology and the emergence of theory pertaining to physiological expression. Among the results of this are the following:

1. The view that language is the result of thinking has fallen out of favour.
2. The theory that language is artificial and the theory that language is natural have been reconciled.

A renaissance in the philology took place in the late 18th century. In the year 1787 the learned Englishman, William Jones, demonstrated the existence of a strong relationship between Sanskrit, Greek, and Latin. In 1808 Karl Wilhelm Friedrich Schlegel argued that the Indian, Persian, Greek, Italian, and German languages belonged to the same linguistic family, which he named the 'Indo-Germanic family'. Comparative studies kept progressing, leading to the establishment of linguistics as an empirical science at the hands of Wilhelm von Humboldt, Jacob Grimm, and Burnouf.[4]

This has had the greatest impact upon the philosophy of language, whose subjects include those general laws which control how some languages are derived from others. It showed how changes occurring to language are subject to laws of inevitability which man cannot possibly alter. This did away with the view of the conventionalists. It made language a natural, living entity which is subject to the laws of life. Max Müller and Ernest Renan were among those who employed philology to explain the formation of language. Müller wanted to make a natural science of language that was subject to natural laws – like blood circulation, for example!

Returning to the issue of the formation of language, let us ask the question: how can philology give us answers to this? Müller believed that there are simple elements in every language which are irreducible; he called these elements 'the roots'. These roots are normally interpreted as being the imitation of sounds occurring in nature, or as an expression of psychological states. However, Müller disregarded these two interpretations, explaining them as universally found within humans, because these origins signify universal meanings. Ultimately, language does not derive from imitation; rather, it stems from man's universal conception of meanings. Before man uttered the word 'cave', for example, he had already conceived the general meaning of 'cavity' which he the applied to the cave. In this way it is possible to reconcile the thought of Locke and Leibniz. As I understand it, Locke claimed that the origin of words is an individuality, while Leibniz argued instead that it was a generality. The word 'cave' is individual as soon as it is applied to this cave or that one, and it is general inasmuch as we do not apply it to this cave or that one until after its general meaning comes to us, which is 'cavity'.

---

4 Mahfouz does not provide a forename for Burnouf. However, the name probably refers to Eugène Burnouf (1801–1852), a French orientalist who made important contributions to the deciphering of Old Persian cuneiform. Mahfouz, Naguib, Hawla l-Adab wa-l-Falsafa, Cairo, 2003, p. 167

So what is the relationship between the concept and the word? Müller responds to this question by saying that it is the idea which inspires the word. This is a primitive law within the mind. Just as physical matter produces a sound if struck, so too the existence of thought produces the word. Like Müller, Renan did not adopt the notion of arbitrariness. However, he did attribute language to imitation, thereby rejecting Müller's notion of universality. According to him, human beings possess a speech faulty which they use of their own accord, and this spontaneity can be attributed to man or his creator. Language is a human feature but is not due to the individual himself; rather, it is due to collective thought. It is the manifest expression of thought and its development.

Physiology was also beneficial in explaining language; it showed that, initially, the purpose of expressive signs was not expression. Charles Bell stated that expressive signs – such as facial movements and changes – are the beginnings of actions whose function is to serve the emotions by giving them expression. They are actions which, by their nature, perpetuate these emotions if they are pleasant, or eliminate them if they are painful. Thereafter they become expressive of these emotions. Darwin shared the views of Charles Bell. However, he used them to interpret the phenomena of expression in a new way which was based upon to three principles:

1. The principle of antithesis.
2. The principle of association with regard to beneficial habits.
3. The principle of effect with regard to the neurological system's influence on the body.

The principle of antithesis explains some of the expressive movements in light of opposition. This is because the final form of a given movement is in opposition to the forms of those movements which accompany emotions that are in opposition to the one expressed by the former. For example, when a cat experiences pleasure it contracts and arches its back. This is because this bearing is opposite to the bearing it assumes if it is in a state of anger or feeling vicious.

According to the principle of useful habits, the parts of the body affect certain movements in order to satisfy an appetite or to perpetuate a feeling. Over the passage of time the performance of these movements becomes a habit. They occur in the body solely for the sake of something – be it an emotion or an appetite – which itself does not require the movement which is occurring. In the case of such states the beneficial value is very little or none at all; however, there remains a value in terms of expression. Many expressive signs are acts which we perform automatically due to habit and hereditary transmission, because our ancestors performed them due to their beneficial aspects. An example of this can be seen in how dogs came to have the habit of licking their offspring in order to clean them. This action, however, is normally accompanied by feelings of affection. It can be traced as a sign their affection to the extent that dogs even lick their human owners.

As for the third principle, this one is independent of the will, and perhaps of habit as well. Its import pertains to the stimulation of the cerebral nerves which generates neural energy. From this, movements and cries are produced, and through the association of meanings they become signs for emotions.

From this we can see that expressive signs did not exist on the basis that they were signs of expression. Rather, they evolved into such though habit, association, and understanding. Thus, there is no reason for the existence of a special trait for speech, as some aforementioned philosophers claimed. Language is subject to natural laws. Words emerge after the discovery of expressive signs and the utilisation of that which is natural and that which is volitional. In terms of their development, words are subject to the laws of thought itself.

In modern times the matter of language turned away from philosophy and logic in favour of sociology and psychology, in particular. On the issue of viewing language as a social phenomenon, this derives from the idea that the sources of language are manifold and infinite. Indeed, what can be known of language is only that which is confined to the conventions of idiomatic usage. But man will only reach the limit, and the extent, of language if its usage spreads and becomes general in the collective society. None of this, however, prevented a psychological interpretation of language. There ended up being an examination of what is known as 'the spirit of language' – that is, an examination of the psyches of peoples as reflected through languages.

The conception of vocal changes as being subject to blind, inevitable laws was abandoned. It was found that the psychological factors – such as imitation or the desire to be understood – exist within the basis of the mechanics of habit which create the expressive signs. If the human being is not aware of vocal changes, this is because they are not a result of thinking, because they are influenced by instinctive enunciation, the enunciation of different peoples. Here the social aspect eclipses the psychological factors.

As for the meanings of words, here the factor is also psychological – it is the thought itself. The meaning of a word is not defined until after it has been used; its meaning is formed through the mentalities of those whose use it. Mentalities, however, differ from one people to another according to culture, era, and modes of thinking. Linguistic developments depict mental developments and, thus, language became the subject of psychological studies. In this way language returned to psychology, and in some ways, to sociology.

From this we can see that the issue of language began with this question: does language convey the truth of things or not? Later it moved on to defining the relationship between thought and language, which of these comes first, and which one produces its counterpart? The solution swings between two views: one which attributes language to a divine source, and another which attributes it to a human source.

Then, with the advancements of comparative philology and physiology, the issue of the source of language was abandoned. It came to be viewed as something living which is subject to the laws of life. It began with contrasting physical movements which developed into signs of expression. Then words appeared and language evolved to express individual racial genius as well as universal human tendencies. At the present time, the subject is monopolised by sociology and psychology.

Art and Culture[1]

We can say, in general, that art is the expression of emotion. This definition is quite sufficient insofar as it isn't biased towards any particular
doctrine of art, nor does it give precedence to any one philosophy of
art over another. The supporters of idealism are those who believe that
art is in the genius of the artist, that it bears his stamp, is characterised
by the mark of his individuality, and is concentrated in his inspirations
and feelings, which are not bound by reality, but greatly transcend it.
They do not dispute that emotion is the cause behind the artist's revelation and the wellspring of his inspirations.

As for the adherents of realism, they restrict the role of art to imitating
the material world and binding it thereto. They don't deny the important and unique agency of emotion in comparing the relative merits
of various artistic imitations, nor do they deny it its due with regard to
its role in pushing the artist towards creativity and mastery. There is
no disagreement concerning the value of emotion and its effect in the
life-blood of beautiful art; however, there is a clear disagreement when
it comes to defining the subject of art. Should art remain pure for the
sake of art, free from anything except emotion and instinct? Or, should
it be possible for art to deal additionally with subjects of the rational
mind, the branches of knowledge, and pronouncements of philosophy
associated with it?

There is an enthusiastic camp of artists and philosophers of pure
art – the art of instinct and of nature. They deem this to be above the

---

1 Article from *al-Majalla al-Jadida* August 1936

goals of rationality and its leanings. They free art from the theories of philosophy and the considerations of such. With regard to music, for example, they believe that the ear of the musician is endowed with a natural gift. It relishes the beauty of the sounds, knows the whereabouts of their harmonies and charms, and from these composes that which enchants the ear. This seizes the junctures of the soul wherein it stirs up an intuitive, instinctive feeling. It does so without a need for this melody to have an intellectual significance that is intended to be conceptualised, conveyed, and so forth. Painting is the result of genius which confers distinction upon the eye of the artist. Such an eye is able, by virtue of what it has been endowed with, to examine the wonderful beauty in colours – both evident and concealed – and to present it in sundry images which delight the eye, please the soul, and in which splendour and bliss pervade. In this manner, literature becomes a simple depiction of natural emotions, such as love, pain, hatred, and pleasure, while anything other than that, i.e., the objectives of the rational mind and its subject matters, will be seen as being in excess of true art, and an addiction to it will degrade its essence and dispossess it of its beauty and its exaltedness.

In order to weigh up and evaluate this opinion, we should define what the mind means, in general. The mind, by dint of its faculties, is the thinking force in the human being. With regard to its expressions and signs, these are the manifold form of knowledge and science. Is it true that the participation of this faulty in the creation of beautiful art is what spoils its beauty and splendour? Is it true that the artist's awareness of these signs of the mind ruins its beauty and reduces its exaltedness?

If, by scientific and intellectual knowledge, the artist seeks to explain – through his art – his theories, to elucidate his intentions, and to reveal his subject matters, then he has strayed from his purpose and deviated from his path, because the first and last aim of the artist is true consciousness, and to give expression to this consciousness beautifully. However, if, through his awareness of science and learned things, the artist wants to expand his horizons, to make a sphere for his consciousness that is greater in terms of loftiness and yearning, and if he desires to give expression to all of this, then he will labour within these parameters, he will remain faithful to his art, and he will create sumptuous art the like of which we have never seen from those artists who shun the mind and knowledge, and who rely solely on instinct and emotion.

Art is the expression of consciousness. Consciousness has its origins in the mingling of psychic forces with the internal life in the mind and the external life in nature and the world. The issue here is not whether his perceptions derive from instinct or education; both are equal in relation to consciousness, and both are connected to its essence inasmuch as life, power, and beauty are within it. It is thus true that the world of the mind – both interior and exterior – opens up before consciousness; it spreads new vitalities through it, and provides it with novel and delightful elements in the spheres of nature and the psyche.

The painter is preoccupied by the colours in flowers, roses, rivers, faces, and the heavens. In these, worlds of perfection and beauty are revealed to him. Now, if an understanding of botany and geology are added to his burning consciousness, it will expand through knowledge of things occurring in nature. Through learning about their ancient and recent histories – the details concerning their historical conditions and phases – he will increase his consciousness in terms of its profundity and its connection to their essences, and these, in turn, will further mingle with his own essence, increase the stirring of his imagination and the awakening of his feelings.

The poet whose soul shines for the love of the sky, and whose senses wander the paths of the celestial spheres, has his radiance glowing brighter and his pride growing more splendorous if he learns, through the science of astronomy, of the lives of these living, infinite celestial spheres and nebula that the speed of light would take millions of years to reach.

In this way, science illuminates the darkness of the mind and uncovers the vaults of its character. It grants literature valuable opportunities for perfection with regard to execution and expression. At first, man did not know anything beyond the irresistible instinct dedicated to preserving his life, the instinct which bound him to his progeny, and the instinct that united him with his tribe. Art is in line with these instincts and emotions; it conveys their meanings and signs. Those who are gifted have the ability to create that which is outstanding and miraculous. Important advances in the sciences, which are studied by man, occurred throughout human history. Sometimes these have occurred due to man's history and culture, sometimes through his relationship to the community in which he lived – that influenced him and which he influenced – and sometimes by that which is related to his being and its peculiarities. Thus, the sphere of knowledge expanded and this facilitated modes of expression. There is no doubt that when someone comprehends these sciences, he increases in the knowledge of consciousness, his mind and his character. Subsequently, if he desires to express himself, he will possess the means to behold what is hidden and see worlds that he would not comprehend anything of were it not for these sciences. The instinctive mind is far baser than that mind whose parts are illuminated by knowledge. The creative output of the former, no matter how talented or equipped with genius, cannot rise above that of the latter if equally equipped with aptitude and talent.

Although it may seem otherwise, I do not mean by this that I prefer intellectual art over the art of instinct; likewise, I cannot say I prefer the instinctual art over intellectual art. Perhaps the distinction between these types of art is exaggerated and the difference is nothing more than an illusion which has no bearing on truth or fact. Art does express emotion, and emotion is conveyed through the nature of the inner psyche and that of external world. This nature, of both the psyche and the world, reveals hidden worlds – worlds not seen with the artless eye – when the light of knowledge is shone on them.

Indeed, there is no instinctive art and intellectual art; rather, art is one in view of its means, and one with regard to its subject. However, this subject may call for the instinctual inclination of the artist, and – aside from this – it may have recourse to works of science and philosophy. Having said all this I cannot now decide in favour of those who support the art of instinct. However, I do concede that ignorance of something is better than familiarity with it, or, that ignorance concerning the truth of a subject matter is what intensifies the strength of our feeling toward it, and increases the beauty and splendour of our expression of it.

In defence of this it may be said that art requires a thin veil of mystery to make it beautiful and enchanting. Learnedness, in its nature, involves knowing the truth and uncovering the mystery – because of this, it fundamentally strips art of its beguiling and magical qualities. The truth is that learning makes the truth of things plain; however, it does not claim – and it cannot claim – that it can elucidate every truth. What we have learned is still but a wave of light on an infinite ocean of darkness.

The function of art is to lift the soul up into the heavens of beauty, to bring the psychic forces of the individual and those of the wider group together in one consciousness, to insert the individuality of the human being into a universal oneness comprising the depths of the earth and the strata of the heavens. The artist will not be accomplishing his task fully unless he creates a connection between his soul, and science and philosophy. If to become educated is the individual duty of the human being in order to ensure that his soul lives in illumination and joy, then it is clearly an offence to prevent the artist from this illumination and joy. The artist is he whose task in life it to spread illumination and joy.

I Have Read (Part 1)[1]

Najib al-Hilali

Democracy consists of manifestations and essence. Its manifestations are elections and a parliament, and its essence is the capability of the people as demonstrated through their education in politics, the soundness of their knowledge concerning their rights and duties, and their general understanding of their role within society. All of these things qualify the people to elect representatives in a manner that is sound, and ensure that the direction they take will be informed by reason. In this way they will be able to see things with a keen and critical eye, to the extent that they will able to newly evaluate what it before them. True democracy, in its nature, aims to educate and train the people – unlike other political doctrines in which governments work to benefit an elite class, or in which they work for the common good according to the viewpoint of an elite class. These latter types of government withhold the light of learning from the people, or only provide it in a narrow and limited way, sometimes under the pretext that treasury funds have dried up, and sometimes under the pretext of the fear of increasing unemployment. The truth which is being concealed is that they are afraid that the people will awaken, and they are anxious about the people becoming enlightened by knowledge and realising that the ruling class is privileged while they are left to occupy a position of inferiority in the darkness of ignorance.

---

1 Article from *al-Ayyam* 30 November 1943

Let's be clear, the real difference between a popular government and an aristocratic government is that the former works for the good of the people and dedicates itself to educating them, engendering confidence, trust and hope. As for the latter, if it does work for the good of the people this is done in a narrow and limited way in order to safeguard its own continuing luxury – above all, this necessitates the exploitation of the people.

In light of all of this we should consider Najib al-Hilali the greatest builder of true democracy in Egypt. He thoroughly understands his role and he completely grasps the importance of his mission. Furthermore, he is endowed with a brilliance in his ability, which reveals to him the right way through the thorns, the difficulties, and the darkness. It is no surprise, therefore, that he yearns for the advancement of a people who are near exhaustion after thousands of years of living under oppression. How often their backs have felt the scourges of violent despots!

I read the minister's report concerning the education of the people and it caused a sense of relief and peace to enter my heart. It lifted me up to the firmament of its most exalted ideals, and it kindled the fire of zeal and virtue in my heart.[2] Through its light I saw the people awakening, as is the desire of this notable minster – a desire so different from that of the oppressors and the despots.

---

2 This is presumably in reference to al-Hilali's *A Report on Educational Reform*, published in 1943.

I Have Read (Part 2)[1]

The Freedom of Genius

Genius is a sublime force. It is characterised by creativity and originality, but can only exist within an atmosphere of absolute freedom.
This doesn't mean that it disapproves of rules; rather, it is a law unto
itself.

I recently read something by a young journalist addressed to Mr el-
Akkad. He was of the opinion that the latter should abandon writing on
his work *A Compilation of Islam's Geniuses* and instead turn his attention to something more worthwhile.[2] Mr el-Akkad responded to him
by saying that the correct and sensible view in this matter is that the
writer is only answerable with regard to the proficiency he has in the
subject, not with regard to his choice of subject. The fact of the matter
is that it is reprehensible and tyrannical that someone would demand
of a writer that he take up those subjects that accord with their taste
– the writer is free to write what he likes and readers is free to read it
or not. The freedom of the writer, as has been mentioned, makes its
own rules. Through his senses the writer is informed of the currents
within the society in which he lives – those which are apparent, but
also those under the surface. He is guided by a sense of freedom in
the choice of his subjects which appear as an expression of the reality

---

1 Article from *al-Ayyam* 7 December 1943

2 The full title of the work being referred to here is *Majmū'atu l-'Abqarīyāti
l-Islāmīyati* by Abbas el-Akkad.

of his environment, as hopes, or as distant dreams put on hold, to be realised in the remote future.

Many a reader will ask: is a history about the genius of Muhammad, Abu Bakr, Umar, and Ali of any real value to us these days? Well I say this: this subject is by no means alien, it is something which stirs the breast of our society. I am not talking here about its religious value or its human significance; rather, I am referring, in particular, to that which connects it with the consciousness of the Arab nation. A universal wakefulness has spread through it which watches over the nation's ancient roots and illuminates its hopes on the horizon. I am calling attention here to the association between its spirit and some of the aspects of our modern Nahda. Those possessing genius are the rightly guided caliphs. They were the rulers who found Islam to be the best expression of the spirit of their era. By this 'spirit' here I mean that noble inclination toward simplicity and equality, or what we refer to as 'the socialism of Islam'.

Socialism is a doctrine of the modern era in Egypt. No party has yet been inclined to stand up for its principles but there is a burning enthusiasm for it in the hearts of many young people. To summarise all this we can say that the freedom of genius is indispensible; it seeks the right way according to its own particular rules and it does not stray from its path.

The Fears of a Writer

In the publication *al-Thaqafa*, one writer wrote a piece warning about embracing the principles of socialism, because, in his view, socialism could only be realised through the shedding of blood. Secondly, he saw it as a threat to intellectual freedom! The reality is that these two charges against socialism couldn't be further from the truth. The foundation of socialism is development, not revolution, as is the case with communism. Many socialist leaders are intellectuals who are famed for their service to the cause of peace – thoughts about shedding blood couldn't be further from the mind of a socialist.

Socialism's advocacy of development is sufficient to refute the erroneous beliefs of those who see it as a threat to human thought.

Advancing the cause of development requires publicity and persuasion within the parameters of the parliamentary system. If socialism attains power through the parliamentary system then it will not consider abolishing it, nor will its esteem for thought and freedom change.

We ask those who are frightened of it: are intellectual freedom and social justice incompatible? Can science and art only originate in a society crippled by poverty, ignorance, and sickness?

Writers should make a distinction between communist dictatorship and democratic socialism. Communism – which calls for revolution – protects itself by means of dictatorship. It permits the existence of only one political party and one point of view, and it eradicates any political parties or views which oppose it. Thought is shackled in a communist state. As for socialism, however, it approves of neither revolution nor dictatorship.

Of Art and History[1]

Umm Kulthum

Umm Kulthum is an incomparable singer – the like of which rarely comes along. Her larynx is of the highest degree; her voice is sweet, melodious, supple and powerful. Her priceless voice is distinguished by its excellent qualities; it combines strength, tenderness, resonance, sweetness, length of breath, and a penetrating impact. Surrounding all of these things is a luminous halo of artistic brilliance whose creative power goes from strength to strength as it continues to charm and enchant. When it astonishes people to the point where they think that there is no further level of astonishment, it then mocks them through its infinite creativity, showing them that there is no limit, nor end, with regard to its power to astonish.

It is undeniable that, among contemporary, Egyptian voices, there is no voice that can compare with the sublime voice of Umm Kulthum. You can praise the singing of Asmahan, of Leila Mourad, and Nur al-Huda, as much as you like, but if you compare their voices to that of Umm Kulthum you do them more harm than good. You abase them though your intention was to exalt them, and you reduce them to the dust thought you sought to raise them to the heavens.

The celebration of life and strength in the songs of Umm Kulthum is such that the songs of other singers, both male and female, fall short of it. Perhaps the artists who compose songs for her are affected by the

1 Article from *al-Ayyam* 21 December 1943

vitality of her spirit and the grace of her voice, such that not a song of hers has ever deviated from the path of true art, be it a song of sorrow or of joy. She remains seated upon her throne. Through her the bright hope of the future is opened to us, while the radiant joys of the past are rolled up.

Zakariyya Ahmad

Zakariyya Ahmad is the indisputable leader of the traditional style. He has a unique station not enjoyed by any other; the musicians of all styles are unanimous in their reverence for him and in their acknowledgment that he produces true art.

There may be a difference of opinion when it comes to the old style of singing and the modern; however, the distinguishing marks of true talent cannot be concealed, regardless of subject or period. It is for this reason that Zakariyya Ahmad is unanimously regarded as a gifted artist. I will not stop here though; instead, I will say this, that among the distinguished contemporary musicians he is the only one who deserves to be called an artist, according to the true meaning of the word. Art is creative ability and originality. These days the notable artists put most of their efforts into borrowing from the music of the West. This is commendable, and it represents a transitional phase, but it is less than art, according to the true sense of the word.

The two outstanding leaders of this movement which leans toward the music of the West are Mohamed El Qasabgi and his brilliant pupil, Mohammed Abdel Wahab. Zakariyya Ahmad, however, is not of their kind; he is truly an artist. His music comes from the bottom of his heart and from the essence of his soul. In some of his songs one might hear the echoes of old songs, but such echoes are natural and arise from his assimilation of the music he studied and benefitted from – in no way do they blot out his own individuality.

As with his great teacher, Sayed Darwish, before him, the art of Zakariyya Ahmad is distinguished by a simplicity which lures emulators, but also an unrelenting impeccability which they cannot hope to attain. Furthermore, it is also distinguished by a realism that is underpinned by genuine expression, to the extent that you can always perceive in his music a perfect harmony between expression and its meaning on the one hand, and their musical interpretation on the other. On top of all this, his songs possess an authentic Egyptian sweetness which causes mutual affection and understanding to burst forth from the depths of our souls; it is almost as if it frankly relates our psychological history with all its shades of joy, passion, contemplation and hope.

It cannot be demanded that artists belong to one particular school or another. All that we can hope from them is that they are proficient and creative. Art is not judged by whether it is old or modern, but by the perfection which flies above the gauges of time.

Concerning the Book *Artistic Imagery in the Qur'an*[1]

I read your book *Artistic Imagery in the Qur'an* with interest and zeal,[2] and I found two great benefits in it. The first benefit is for the reader, especially the reader who has not had the good fortune of studying the Islamic sciences nor of plunging into the mysteries of its eloquence. But there is no doubt that even the erudite reader will find new illumination and exceptional enjoyment in your book. An eternal book like the Qur'an does not reveal all of its aesthetic secrets to one generation, no matter how refined its taste or keen its understanding. The present generation has its own task in this matter, just as future generations will have theirs. The important point is that you have succeeded in becoming a voice for our current generation, with regards to carrying out of this beautiful and sublime duty. Our generation seeks the aid of such highly artistic works which are being composed by its contemporaries who enter into the valley of art guided by their light.

From an aesthetic point of view, our era is truly the era of music, of image making, and the story. It is you who, with vigour and inspiration, show us that our beloved Qur'an is the music, the imagery, and the story, at their most sublime forms in terms of inspiration and

---

1 Article from *al-Risala* 23 April 1945

2 This piece represents an open letter addressed to Sayyid Qutb (1906–1966) following the publication of his book *Artistic Imagery in the Qur'an* in 1945. The book is largely a work of literary criticism and differs markedly from Qutb's later, more radical, works.

creativity. Have we not read the Qur'an before? Certainly we have, and memorised some of its chapters and verses in happy times gone by. The Qur'an gave me – and continues to give me – faith in my heart and enchantment in my soul. Yet, although we feel that mysterious and inscrutable enchantment through our senses, and though our consciences are deeply touched by it, nevertheless, our minds cannot comprehend it nor can perception reach it. It is like the melody of a singer, of which, those who listen to it know neither how nor why it fills them with delight. Your book arrives like a spiritual guide for the Arab listeners and readers of our generation; it takes them to regions of loveliness and places of beauty, and reveals to them the mysteries of enchantment and the charms of creation. The Qur'an was in the heart, but now it fills up the heart, the eye, the ear, and the mind, altogether. After much reflection and contemplation you stated that:

> The use of imagery is the favoured device in the style of the Qur'an.
> Through images that can be sensed and imagined it expresses
> themes, psychological states, tangible events, visual scenes, human
> characters, and human nature. Then, it rises up through the images it
> paints, giving them new life or movement. The themes assume form
> or movement, the psychological state becomes a picture or a scene,
> the human character becomes a living personality, and human
> nature become corporeal and visible...

You then proceeded to cite examples of each case, interpreting, explaining, and clarifying as you went. You were not content with that alone, however, for with great energy you also began to investigate the foundations upon which this miraculous imagery rests – the sensual dramatisation and anthropomorphism – with an abundance of examples and quotations. But you were not content with the enchantment of this divine abundance with which God had imbued you, for you stated that, 'If we say that image making is the fundamental basis of expression in the Qur'an, and that dramatisation and anthropomorphism are the two distinctive phenomena in this image making, this in no way means that we have attained the utmost extent with regard to elucidating the special characteristics of the Qur'an, in general, nor with regard to the special characteristics of Qur'anic imagery, in particular … there is a harmony that attains its apex in the imagery of the Qur'an.' Through this section you, yourself, attain the apex of literary criticism, taste, and insight.

I would have liked to cite some of what appears in your book concerning the practical critique of Qur'anic verses, but my brief remarks would be inadequate and I am disinclined to do so for one who disdains, under any circumstances, to compare verses of the Qur'an on the basis of literary merit. Nevertheless, I should acknowledge here that in the two sections entitled 'Artistic Harmony' and 'Narrative in the Qur'an' the Qur'an has blessed your efforts. It has exalted you to a height which would be impossible for a literary critic to attain without its blessing!

Now, with regard to the second benefit, this belongs to you! This is because the book as a whole manifests your talent as a literary critic. You have the ability to express the way in which the text affects you in the most beautiful manner. But you do not stop there; you go further, elucidating the sites of beauty within the text itself, as well as the music, imagery, and life, which adorn it. You then examine the music, its melodies and its varieties; you investigate the imagery, its colours and its shades; you seek the life therein, its warmth and movement. And still you do not content yourself with all of this! Your mind connects text with text until you find a oneness behind the signs and a universal system behind the verses. You make the book into a living being which possesses a clear purpose, a brilliant guiding principle, and a plan in place. You aim for artistic inimitability in every way and you attain it out of worthiness; you have a beautiful sensibility, a level of taste which is difficult to attain, and a manner of thinking which bears the perfume of philosophy.

Now, allow me to address a question and to make an observation. My question is this: you speak of the production of imagery, of dramatisation, of anthropomorphism, and of artistic harmony – all of which are the spirit of poetry and its quintessence, before being anything else – but did it not occur to you that you were imposing limitations on the type of language in the Qur'an during the course of this investigation of yours?

Now, as for my observation, this concerns the section which you devoted to human types. I found therein, in the verses which you cited, that which expresses human qualities and psychological traits, but not human types. The term 'human type', in the correct sense, represents something that possesses a broader meaning than this. It comprises human qualities, but it may also involve more than this. The important thing is that types exhibit qualities in such a way that is consistent with their particular temperaments. Human types are recognised as having limits, irrespective of the difference in how they are classified by psychologists. Qualities, on the other hand, have no such restriction placed on them. Perhaps you meant 'qualities' rather than 'types'!